I think all women struggle with fear on ‹[...] part of our spirit as we realize how precious and fragile life can be. With her relatable, humorous, and warm writing style, Hallie Lord manages to encourage, challenge, and, most importantly, make you feel normal. Pick this book up today and get ready for a fun ride. You will find yourself nodding your head, laughing out loud, and breathing a big sigh of relief that it's all going to be okay.

— Melanie Shankle, *New York Times* best-selling author
of *Nobody's Cuter Than You*

The deeply personal stories Hallie Lord shares are humorous, fun, and delightful — yet packed with jaw-dropping insights. It is not an exaggeration to say that this book will change your life.

— Jennifer Fulwiler, SiriusXM radio host and bestselling
author of *Something Other than God*

Hallie Lord is a gifted and graceful writer whose wisdom is hard-won — and all the more compelling as a result. For women struggling to replace fear with faith, this intimate, funny, and poignant account of Hallie's own struggle offers a road map toward peace, from an author who feels like a friend.

— Colleen Carroll Campbell, journalist, former presidential
speechwriter, and author of *My Sisters the Saints:
A Spiritual Memoir* and *The New Faithful:
Why Young Adults Are Embracing Christian Orthodoxy*

Jesus said, "Be not afraid." St. John Paul II said, "Be not afraid." But I'm afraid to say … I still have lots of fears in life. After reading this book, Hallie Lord will be the third voice in my head reminding me to "be not afraid" and to trust in God. Thanks Jesus, JPII, and Hallie!

— Lino Rulli, host of *The Catholic Guy* show on SiriusXM Satellite Radio

Hallie Lord goes toe-to-toe with fear and provides a witty and fearless response in the face of such challenges today. *On the Other Side of Fear: How I Found Peace* is a remarkably truthful book that not only encourages us but also illuminates the sources behind many fears today in order to root them out and live fearlessly in and with Christ.

— Leah Darrow, author of *Decent Exposure* and former ɲ
on *America's Next To⸍*

In a culture awash (and adrift) in marginally helpful selᶠ
Hallie Lord truly has launched into the deep with thiꜱ
brims with practical advice and gracious personal
all who (like all of us) struggle at times with fear

— Patᵢ

"Do not fear; only believe" (Lk 8:50). When we hear these words of Jesus, we may well reply, "Yes, Lord — but how?" In this wise and witty book, Hallie Lord offers penetrating, practical insights from years of struggle with fear in its various forms. In the end, her personal victories over anxiety powerfully illustrate the biblical truth that "there is no fear in love" (1 Jn 4:18).

— Paul Thigpen, author of *Manual for Spiritual Warfare*

The Bible is filled with encouragement to not be afraid. It's the first command of every angel and the first words spoken by Jesus on Easter. Yet how hard it is! In this wonderfully uplifting book, Hallie Lord shows us how to tap into the strong confidence of faith to conquer our daily concerns. She doesn't ignore fear, which can never be banished, but confronts it and reveals how we can loosen its grip. Vulnerable, poignant, and inspiring, this is the book you need if you've ever been worried or unsure about life.

— Brandon Vogt, author of *Return: How to Draw Your Child Back to the Church*

On the Other Side of Fear
How I Found Peace

ON THE OTHER SIDE OF FEAR

HOW I FOUND *Peace*

HALLIE LORD

Our Sunday Visitor

www.osv.com
Our Sunday Visitor Publishing Division
Our Sunday Visitor, Inc.
Huntington, Indiana 46750

Our Sunday Visitor Publishing Division, Our Sunday Visitor, Inc., 200 Noll Plaza, Huntington, IN 46750; 1-800-348-2440.

ISBN: 978-1-61278-966-8 (Inventory No. T1730)
eISBN: 978-1-61278-972-9
LCCN: 2016945383

Cover design: Lindsey Riesen
Cover art: Shutterstock

PRINTED IN THE UNITED STATES OF AMERICA

To Dan, who kept telling me that we had nothing to fear — even if we ended up living under a bridge — because we have each other and because God will never abandon us. I laughed, but now I believe. Thank you, my love.

And to my Opa, who taught me the value of courage every time he challenged me to undertake a Feat of Bravery. I miss you.

What if I fall?
Oh, but my darling,
what if you fly?
— e.h.

CONTENTS

Introduction

When I was thirty-six weeks pregnant with my fifth child, a little girl we named Zelie Olive, my husband walked through the back door of our cottage by the sea as I was cleaning the lunch dishes, with comments about getting off work early that day quick to his lips. He ushered me to bed so that I could nap, but sleep proved elusive. I knew, the way husbands and wives just know after having been married for almost a decade, that there was something he wasn't telling me.

Later that night, after our little ones were tucked soundly into their beds, sandy traces of the salty sea still sticking to their toes, he sat me down and broke the news. Earlier that day he had been laid off, effective immediately. His company, he explained, had become the latest victim of the financial crisis that had hit the Gulf Coast as a result of the Deepwater Horizon oil spill. We were left with two weeks severance pay and less than a month of insurance to our name.

I spent the last weeks of my pregnancy curled up in a ball on our living room couch. My children took turns cuddling up with me, releasing the silly things that had been dancing in their heads into my ear, and kissing their newest sibling as she rolled and stretched beneath my ribs. My sweet husband brought me food, rubbed my feet, and assured me that we would be fine. Friends and family visited and poured love into our family in myriad ways as the summer grew later and hotter.

It was a beautiful, life-giving, love-rich time, but I barely experienced any of it. I had locked myself away in a dungeon of fear and anxiety, where my only companions were vivid worst-case scenarios that played in my head on repeat. I closed my eyes against the rays of light that attempted to break through the small prison window and silenced the voices that were calling out to me with words of comfort and reassurance.

****

When we are in danger, our instinct is to run and hide and then to curl up in a ball to protect ourselves from being hurt. That is the same instinct we tap into when we're afraid. We hide away and then turn in on ourselves and wait, head down and knees in, until the pummeling stops. Do we escape some of fear's more vicious blows when we do that? Perhaps. But we will never win the war that way. No one ever defeated their fears by hiding from them.

Do you know why fear stands behind you and whispers scary things into your ear? Because it doesn't want you to look it in the face. It knows that the moment you stand up and engage, you will discover what it has desperately been trying to hide from you. You will discover that fear is a liar.

Fear paints vivid pictures of problems without solutions, sorrow without relief, mortification without mercy, and life without joy. It tells us that there is no hope and that our burdens are too heavy for any one person to endure. Admittedly, it does so in a very compelling way. But "compelling" is not synonymous with "true," so these lies can only thrive when we push them down deep inside and hide them from the light.

This book is the story of how I looked fear in the face and discovered that its power is an illusion, definitively destroyed when held up to the light of God.

The following chapters can stand alone as each one possesses its own unique lesson. You can read this book from front to back or back to front or you can skip around. It can be consumed in one sitting, or fifty. You can even read it while standing on your head, if you like. It's up to you.

No matter how you approach this book, though, I can promise you one thing: you will walk away from it knowing how to conquer your fears. It won't happen overnight, and it will require a good deal of discipline, fortitude, and faith, but you will never regret having taken the journey. I wasted far too many years in the grip of fear, and I can tell you that no matter what it takes to overcome your fears, no matter how hard you have to work or how much you have to sacrifice, it's worth it. For here, on the other side of fear, lies freedom. Here lies the ability to love, savor, and create with abandon. And here lies the vibrant, adventurous, full life that God has created just for you.

Welcome, sweet friends.

CHAPTER ONE

Champagne Flutes

Fear is the enemy of love.

~ St. Augustine

For our wedding, Dan and I received a pair of champagne flutes. They were delicate and perfectly shaped, and I loved them. I loved them so much, in fact, that one night, having moved into a new home earlier that day, I pounded on the door of our old house and asked the bewildered new owners if I might peer into their kitchen cabinets to see if I'd left them behind in the move.

It was November, or maybe December, but definitely post-Daylight Saving Time, and the evening was cold, dark, and rainy. I must have looked a sight with my long coat pulled tightly over my ratty moving clothes and my wet hair stuck to the side of my face. I didn't have their phone number, though, and was desperately afraid that they'd throw them out or give them away before I had a chance to retrieve them, so there I stood, pounding away with a slightly manic look in my eye.

They let me in, and there, tucked into the back of a worn wooden cupboard, sat my two perfect matching flutes. I quickly tucked them under my arm and hurried out of the home that was no longer mine with grateful thanks and mildly mortified apologies on my lips.

That twenty-four-year-old newlywed would never have believed you had you told her that five years later she would be furiously smashing those same glasses into a million shining shards against her kitchen sink.

FEATS OF BRAVERY

You do things in a marriage that you never expect you'll do. You become a person that you never thought you'd become. Most of the time this is a good thing. Marriage has a way of making you more generous and selfless and generally less wrapped up in yourself. But that doesn't happen by accident. That happens because marriage refines you by fire, and fire is hot, and fire burns, and if you have any kind of sense of self-preservation, you spend a lot of time wondering how you can escape this painful refining process. Not escape the marriage, but maybe find a way to make it hurt a little less. Or ask not quite so much of you. Or be satisfied with less than your all and everything.

The smashing of the wine glasses was my way of telling God to back off and give Dan and me a break. From Dan's perspective it probably looked more like his wife had become a raging lunatic hell-bent on spewing the worst kind of vitriol in his direction, but at the heart of it my grievance wasn't with him; it was (though I didn't realize it at the time) with God. The God who had allowed relentless brutal financial struggles to mark our first years together. The God who held back the relief I thought we'd been promised. The God who had stood silently by and watched as the brave, fearless girl I'd been raised to be became a controlling, terrified shadow of herself.

When my mother was young, my grandfather started a family tradition called "Feats of Bravery." That thing you are scared to do? You will do it, and you will do it with pluck because it's a Feat of Bravery. You will cross the log that bisects the river, climb to the very top of the waterfall, and jump into the icy-cold mountain stream because you are brave all the way deep down into your bones and no log, waterfall, or mountain stream could possibly take that away from you. In fact, the opposite was considered true — these challenges actually served to encourage and strengthen you. This pursuit, and subsequent acquisition, of fearlessness was at the heart of our family culture, and I loved it.

And then somehow I lost it. I went from being a young woman who courageously backpacked through Europe, proudly assembled her own furniture, and adventurously drove solo across the country to a (somewhat less) young woman who felt utterly paralyzed by fear and anxiety. With every furious strike of glass against my metal sink, with every anguished cry, and with every hot, salty tear that rolled down my cheek, I was mourning the woman I'd been and begging God to give her back to me.

I sunk down onto the hard, cold tile and struggled for breath as Dan grabbed his keys and walked out the front door without a word. He was tired. I was tired. Our union was tired. My newly acquired anxiety, not content to stay tucked away inside me, increasing my heart rate and stealing my breath, had crept out and begun to poison my marriage.

I don't know how most people handle anxiety, but my response was to try to control whatever circumstances of life fell under my jurisdiction. The problem was that many of the things that fell under my jurisdiction also fell under Dan's jurisdiction and were, in fact, meant to be co-managed by the two of us. As I saw it, though, when your ship is going down, you can't have two captains, and I couldn't stand the thought of anyone being at the helm of our sinking ship but me. That sounds prideful, and to some degree it was, I'm sure, but it was more of a gut-level response to feeling that our life was spinning out of control and that I needed to cling to whatever pieces I could still command. All my husband could see, though, was that I was casting a more emphatic vote of No Confidence in him with each and every passing day.

I pulled myself off the ground and headed for my cold, empty bed. As was always the case after one of our increasingly frequent battles, the minute Dan left, all of my fury and resentment almost instantaneously dissipated leaving me bereft, full of regret, and longing for the comfort of his strong arms and familiar shoulders.

I reached into the top drawers of my mahogany bed-side table, pulled out a well-worn See's floral candy box, sat it on my lap, and pulled off the top. Inside were almost a hundred handwritten letters that Dan had given me over the years. It had become my tradition to read a handful of them after almost every fight, when we were apart for any extended period of time, and anytime I needed to be re-minded of what was at the core of our union when you beat back the briars of weariness and frustration.

At the top of the pile was a journal entry Dan had composed about the two of us shortly after we'd met:

> Cars may wreck around us, stocks may rise and fall, clocks wind down, but it's not enough to distract us from each other as we chatter and ask and talk like two parts of a steamroller engine. I touch her and she touches back. She cares about me. She encourages me. She likes me, not for certain things I do, but precisely for what I am. I am what she loves. And she is what I love. How about that?

A heart-wrenching realization washed over me: I didn't think Dan could write those same words honestly anymore. We no longer acted like two parts of a steamroller engine. I no longer encouraged him. And did he still know how deeply I loved him for precisely what he was and not what he did?

How could he when all I ever did was to correct, suggest, micromanage, and fret? What had happened to the carefree girl who loved with abandon and wanted nothing more than to make him feel beloved by her? And how could I fix it? How do you pull yourself out of a downward spiral when you feel so unbearably sad and paralyzingly afraid? How do you wrestle a sinking ship out of a storm when all your strength is gone?

The answer came quickly. "You pour love in, my sweet girl. So much love that it drives out all the fear. Every last bit of it."

Call it divine inspiration, a whisper from the Holy Spirit, a gentle nudge from our heavenly Father — or all of the above, I suppose — but even before I knew exactly what this prompting meant or how to go about answering it, I knew that this was what I must do. I knew without a shadow of a doubt that I must summon all the love I possessed, borrow a whole lot more from God, and pour it all into Dan. I had to silence the fearful voices in my head, refuse to allow them access to my voice, and strip them of their power over us.

The old me would have immediately started arguing with God and listing my objections. This marriage was a partnership, why should I suddenly stop sharing my perspective on things? What about the Scriptural exhortation to admonish my brother when he sinned? Was Dan being exhorted to do the same? Once upon a time I would have certainly hoped so.

I was so tired of being a resounding gong and clanging cymbal, though, that I was willing to try anything, even embracing the "if you don't have anything nice to say, don't say anything at all" adage of my youth. I knew that God wasn't asking me to become a Stepford Wife, he was simply offering me a formula — a temporary corrective measure, if you will — for overcoming my fears and healing my marriage. A formula that didn't just ask me to bite my tongue, but demanded that I fill the void with love. He knew that I needed to experience for myself the truth that darkness and light cannot coexist.

I sat in the darkness, pondering how to answer this call. Pies were definitely in order, as were love letters, tokens of affection, and actual affection, of course. I was about to switch my lamp back on and begin making a list when Dan's headlights swam across our bedroom walls. I heard his key in the lock, held my breath, and prayed that God would help us find our way back to peace.

Moments later Dan crawled into bed and wrapped his arms around me and I knew. I knew that though I had a lot of work to do and that together we had a long way to go, we were going to be fine. Even better than fine.

TESTED COURAGE

The months that followed were not easy. Every day I searched the pantry for random ingredients that I could turn into a meal, and I considered adding the customer service representatives at the utility companies to my Christmas card list for the number of times I had to call and beg them to hold off on disconnecting our utilities. As serious financial difficulties continued to plague us, my newly assigned mission to love often stung. Even with the consolation I'd received from God, the shedding of my controlling nature caused more than a few growing pains.

To say that I did this imperfectly would be a huge understatement. But amidst those growing pains I could see that the roots of our marital tree were growing deeper and stronger and that tiny blossoms that promised rich fruit had sprung forth. Our arguments began to decrease in frequency and were replaced by sweet moments of romance and rebonding.

On some level this didn't surprise me. It serves to reason that if you start treating your spouse better, your relationship will thrive. What did surprise me was that the previously implacable grips of fear that had imprisoned me for the last handful of years had slowly begun to release their hold on me.

I couldn't see it at the time, but my putting a stop to the endless cycle of criticism allowed Dan to get off the defensive and return all of the love I was pouring into him, often tenfold. God parted the storm clouds, and I was able to see, once again, how much this man loved me. I was reminded by his every sacrifice (which were daily and plenty) that he would, in fact, do anything and everything within his power to care and provide for me.

Yes, we'd been threatened with eviction. Yes, our utilities were sometimes turned off. Yes, we were without insurance. Yes, we both worried about providing for the needs of our children, but what I began to see is that the entire time that I'd felt the need to micromanage our lives, Dan was doing everything possible to bring us to greener pastures. He was hustling like no man has ever hustled, working two, sometimes three jobs at a time, and humbling himself to borrow money when life demanded it. My fretful contribution had added nothing but animosity.

Do you know who was behind the fact that we struggled? God. With sudden clarity I realized that God had allowed these circumstances. It was he who had brought us to this season of want and allowed us to suffer. He had tied these crosses to our back and asked us to carry them. And though I hadn't wanted to admit it at the time, we had consented. As we were preparing for marriage, Dan and I had told God that we would follow him wherever he led, through rocky valleys and beautiful vistas. We wanted to do his will, trusting in his goodness. Well, as it turned out, his will was to remake us in his image, and his method was poverty. And to give credit where credit is due, it was effective.

God is endlessly creative and has an infinite number of ways to purify a soul. He could see that Dan and I had become far too reliant on, and proud of, our own abilities. Poverty is a surprisingly potent antidote to such a weakness. When all of your efforts to earn your daily bread prove fruitless, you quickly start begging God for help. And after enough of this begging, you begin to see (and have to concede) that everything ultimately flows from him, not you. That's humbling.

The wonderful thing about God is that he's always waiting to offer consolation and insight right at that very moment when you feel your knees start to buckle from the weight of it all. Every so often during this painful process he would part the curtains that hung behind his workshop windows and allow us to peer in, just for a moment, so that we could see how he'd been softening our hearts while pummeling away with his mallet. We could see that he'd somehow managed to make us a little more patient, a bit more kind, and a lot more humble.

That young woman who'd traveled solo around the world had an adventurous spirit, absolutely, but courageous? Only until she was tested, and then that "courage" crumbled so quickly you would have missed it if you'd blinked. She marched through life never once giving credit to God for her accomplishments, never thanking him for her gifts.

PIES AND PEPPERMINT

There's a very satisfying high that comes from doing daring things. And I absolutely agree with my family's assessment that challenges such as Feats of Bravery can serve to strengthen a person. But this brand of courage ultimately needs to be supported by valor, a sort of undaunted courage in the face of overwhelming odds. The kind of valor that comes from trusting God implicitly and knowing that he will never abandon you though the winds may batter and the waves crash upon you. The kind of valor that is free of pride and posturing. The kind of valor that knows that what God says is true — that strength is found in weakness.

I had become a victim of fear because I believed that everything depended on me and that the only way to overcome my anxieties was to assert control. Oh, how wrong I was. All along freedom had been waiting for me to meet fear head-on with love.

When I was worried about buying groceries, I found peace in taking our last box of cherry jello, preparing it lovingly, and serving it to our kids on our very best china.

When Dan seemed especially stressed about paying the bills, I found solace in lovingly rubbing his back, encouraging him, and thanking God that we'd been given the privilege of carrying this cross together.

When I was utterly weary from the challenges that come with a bank account that hates you, I found relief in praying for the poor, meditating on their suffering, and giving thanks to God for the many gifts he'd given us.

I was not then, nor am I now, perfect at this practice, but I suspect that if one could measure such a thing, we'd find that the degree to which we pour love into our lives and loved ones is the degree to which fear is forced out.

Someone once told me that if you pray for your enemies, you will no longer be able to hate them. That the moment you begin to advocate for goodness in their life is the same moment that your animosity will begin to exhaust. This is because the light of love and the darkness of hatred cannot possibly exist in the same space.

The same is true of love and fear.

Love creates life-affirming beauty, fear sets out to destroy it. Love is joyful, fear miserable. Love frees, fear imprisons. Love is kind, fear cruel. Love is honest, fear deceitful. Love is brave, fear afraid. And love is strong, while fear is weak.

For as long as we exist on this earthly planet, love and fear will be at war. There is no harmony to be found between the two. But though they may do battle over and over again, love's victory is written in the stars. For love is God, and God is love, and both are omnipotent.

Later that year, on the Feast of the Holy Family, Dan handed me another letter for my See's candy box. This one told the story of a family that was still young and had much to learn, but was working hard every day to choose love over fear and because of it had never been happier:

> So, here on the Feast of the Holy Family, we heard in Mass how, after Jesus was born, an angel told Joseph to take his little family and live in Egypt so King Herod would not find them.

They were there for about a year or two before Herod died and they could safely return to Joseph's home in Nazareth.

And what did they do in Egypt? No one knows. But I know what we would have done, if it had been us. Knowing that we couldn't leave — not yet — because God needed us to stay there for a little while, I would have gotten a job teaching theology. We would have chosen a small mud and brick house in the sub-suburbs where our neighbors periodically crept by quietly on chariots and sketched drawings of our house to turn in to the neighborhood housing board as proof that we weren't combing the sand on our property as often as everybody would like.

It would never rain, we would be exhausted and overworked, we would never see our families back in Palestine, and we would rarely have any shekels to spend since theology teachers don't make much.

But we would settle in. And Christmas would come. And I would fret a little about how few presents we could buy. But you know what? I would be happy. I would be happier than I'd ever been in my life. How would that be possible?

The broad answer is that all things are possible for God. More specifically, I would look at our Christmas tree, festooned with baubles and glistening with colored lights (a miracle, and not because no one had discovered electricity, but because we had not paid our power bill and our service had not been disconnected). I would see the lights gleaming in the eyes of our children who, for all our lack of shekels, looked somehow healthy, and warm, and well-fed. I would look at my wife, plump with a new baby, smiling her beautiful smile, holding wrapped presents for the kids. I would smell baked pies and peppermint and chocolate, and drink wine, and kiss my wife on her soft, full lips and think what a magnificent thing it was that God had brought so much out of an exile in the desert.

That's how it would be with us, if an angel told us we had to go to Egypt. Thank God we get to stay here.

Dan and Hallie were back. They had much to learn and many mountains yet to climb, but they were back.

CHAPTER TWO

Trail Mix

But God doesn't call us to be comfortable. He calls us
to trust Him so completely that we are unafraid to put
ourselves in situations where we will be in trouble
if He doesn't come through.

~ *Francis Chan*

If you've never been to Alabama in the summer — never
had your glasses fog up the minute you stepped out your
front door, wondered whether you had merely imagined
that phenomenon known as "wind," or had your makeup
literally melt off your face — you should know that it is hot.
And humid. And possibly not fit for human habitation.
Which is not to say that I don't have a soft spot for it in my
heart, because I most definitely do, but — oh my word — is
it hot.

Even by Alabama standards, though, it was scorch-
ing the day I buckled my four young children into their
car seats and headed for Point Clear. We were on our way
to the Grand Hotel, where my mother, caring more about
spending time with her grandchildren than, say, actually
surviving to see her sixtieth birthday, was waiting for us
to join her.

We were about to pull onto I-10 and head across Mobile Bay when something on the side of the road caught my

eye. Unthinkingly, or perhaps prompted by a force I could not see, I pulled over.

I put my car into park and took my foot off the brake. Less than ten yards away from me were three men in long heavy gray robes. They appeared to be perched quite contentedly in the blazing sun atop a guard rail. They turned their heads in my direction, and as their eyes met mine, their faces broke into wide, ebullient smiles.

I got out of my car and walked over to them. They introduced themselves to me, sharing that they were friars from a small Dominican community in France called The Little Brothers of the Lamb. I've always had an affinity for French people, having no small amount of French blood running through my own veins, and was tickled to hear the signature French lilt that marked the edges of their vowels. They were on their way, they said, to help the Little Sisters of the Lamb build a monastery in Kansas City and, having taken a vow of extreme poverty, were at the mercy of whatever motorists offered to take them a few miles down the road.

I laughed and said that while I would have loved to be able to help them, I was headed in the opposite direction. Their faces lit up with childlike glee, they grabbed their backpacks, and, talking over one another like giddy children, all assured me that it was no problem at all because they had every faith that I'd been sent by God and that their next ride was waiting wherever I dropped them next.

These days I drive an enormous van that can fit all nine of our family members (plus another handful of poor souls who make the questionable decision to travel with us), but back then I drove a very small two-door Saturn that already had four children stuffed into it. I was about to stammer an apology in the hopes of stopping them in their enthusiastic tracks when all of a sudden I remembered a story that I'd read about Mother Angelica, the nun who founded the international television network EWTN with not a penny to her name and no media experience.

Before she had a television network, she was called by God to start a small publishing house that printed short pamphlets of an evangelical nature. Somehow she'd gotten her hands on a small printing press that was to be delivered to her monastery. When the men delivering the printing press arrived, they took one look at Mother Angelica's entryway, pulled out their measuring tapes to confirm, and told her that, sadly, the printing press wouldn't fit through her door.

Not being a woman easily deterred, she responded, "Well, of course it will fit through my door! God sent it to me!" She told the men that she and her sisters were going to go to the chapel to pray for God's assistance and that she had every faith (and expectation) that when they returned, the printing press would be inside her building.

They tried to argue with her, but she would have none of it, turned on her heel, and marched to the chapel. There she told God that she would need him to temporarily change the laws of physics so that his gift could be put to good use, please and thank you. When she returned, sure enough, the printing press was in the building and the men left utterly speechless for they had no explanation for how they'd managed to get that printing press through her door. But Mother Angelica knew. God had worked a little miracle just for her and just as she knew he would.

I glanced at my tiny car, looked at the three full-grown men happily ambling in its direction, and thought, "Okay, God. If you want me to give these men a ride, you make them fit." Somehow I knew that he would.

There are moments in life, rare moments, when the Holy Spirit descends and suggests so strongly that you do something that the space between your will and God's becomes startlingly thin. Sometimes I can't help but think that if that mystical space became manifest, and we could see it with our flawed human eyes, we would find that it is as translucent as batiste. This was one of those moments. I knew like I've rarely known anything in my life that I was meant to give these men a ride to, as they put it, wherever their next ride was waiting for them.

They tossed their backpacks into my trunk and began to fold themselves, one after another, into my car. By the time I climbed into the driver's seat, the friars were chattering away with my giggling children. Though to this day I could not draw you a diagram of how we all managed to fit ourselves into that car, somehow we did.

CAN YOU FEEL IT NOW?

I pulled my car back onto the road, headed across Mobile Bay, and began what was one of the most spiritually profound experiences of my life. As Dan so eloquently put it once, as soon as the three friars joined us, a "spiritual fizz" filled the car. We didn't discuss anything particularly profound — though their tales of their journey thus far were entertaining and the way in which they encouraged me in my vocation was hugely uplifting. It wasn't just that these men were joyful, though they absolutely were. The best way I can think to describe it is to say that it was as if somehow the Holy Spirit himself had managed to squeeze himself into my car as well.

Never before, and never since, have I felt the presence of God so intensely. I wish I could have bottled that experience so that everyone could get a taste of what those thirty minutes spent in the presence of those friars felt like, but even then, I doubt words could adequately describe the experience. Simply put: it was otherworldly.

Our time together passed swiftly, and before I knew it, they were climbing back out of my car. Though, at that time, my bank account spent more time in the red than not, I felt compelled to offer them what little cash I had in my wallet. Due to their vow of poverty, though, they refused to accept it. I frantically searched my car looking for anything I might offer to help sustain them on their journey, but all I could find was a half-eaten bag of trail mix. I sheepishly asked whether they might want the last of it, to which, with twinkling eyes, they responded, "Oh, yes! Absolutely! Does it have M&Ms in it, by any chance?" Oh, that you could have seen the looks of glee that danced across their faces when I assured them that yes, of course, it had M&Ms.

Right as I was about to climb back in my car and continue on down the road, they humbly asked whether I might allow them to surround my car and sing the hymn "May God Bless You and Keep You" to my children and me. They began to sing, and I started to cry. I cried while they sang. I cried while I hugged them good-bye. I cried as I drove away. And I kept crying as I called my husband to share with him what had just happened to me.

For years Dan and I had been experiencing relentless trials — financial trials, marital trials, extended family trials, and more — and I'd begun to think that maybe God didn't love me. Or rather that he did love me, but that I'd cut myself off from that love, being the terrible person that I am. What else could explain his silence? Why else would he withhold relief and comfort? But then he sent his friars to me, somehow managed to fit them all into my tiny car, and allowed me the privilege of spending thirty life-changing minutes in their God-soaked presence. Minutes during which God chanted, "I love you, my daughter. I love you. Can you feel it now?"

People talk about mystical experiences and try to explain them because when something that awesome occurs, you want to share it with the entire world. But they, and now I, always sound a little crazy because God's a little crazy, and when he deigns to reach down from heaven and touch the earth, crazy things happen. And those crazy things don't fit easily into flawed human language. All I can say is that was the day that I went from thinking that God was probably real and that he probably loved me to knowing that he is exactly who he says he is and believing completely that he absolutely loves me. That was the "before and after" moment of my life.

After I finally stopped crying, I started to think about those three friars and wonder what it was that they knew that I didn't. Here they were in a foreign country, with no money, no car, no home, and no real plan other than to somehow hitchhike hundreds of miles until they landed in Kansas City, and yet they could not possibly have been more joyful or at peace. I, on the other hand, had a car, a roof over my head, and at least a small income, and yet I was full of fear and anxiety and had little joy and even less peace. What was I missing? Did God favor these three men more than he favored me? Or was it, perhaps, that they knew some secret that I had yet to stumble upon?

I figured, as long as God was touching the earth and doing crazy things, I might as well ask him. Almost immediately — as he likes to take advantage of my attention when he has it — a scene from a few months earlier popped into my mind.

I had been fretting about money, and Dan kept telling me that everything was going to be fine. Over and over again I replied, "But you can't know that! You have no idea what the future holds!" Finally I added (with no small amount of histrionics), "For all you know we could all end up living under a bridge!" Do you know what he said? He said, "You're right, Hallie. We could end up living under a bridge. But even if we did, we'd be okay because we'd have each other and God would be with us."

And that was the end of that conversation. Because there's no point in arguing with an insane person.

I'm starting to think insane people are God's favorite kind of people because he played that scene for me in Technicolor and whispered, "Dan's right, you know. He knows what those friars know. As long as I am with you, you will have everything you need regardless of whether you live in a mansion or under a bridge."

That ebullience the monks possessed? They possessed it because they weren't afraid of living under a bridge or on the side of the road. They weren't afraid of going hungry or only eating one half of a bag of trail mix shared between them for an entire day. They didn't fear rain, or cold, or the merciless Alabama heat. They carried God with them wherever they went. And so, in a way that is simultaneously utterly mysterious and breathtakingly simple, they were at peace.

 CHAPTER THREE

Spark

Do something beautiful for God.
Do it with your life.
Do it every day. Do it in your own way.
But do it!

~ St. Teresa of Calcutta

My husband is a natural father. Of the two of us, he is the better parent. He's the perfect balance of playfulness and firm guiding hand and never even blinks at the idea of watching our seven small scrumptious children all on his own. When he leaves town, I batten down the hatches and warn the children of all the ghastly things I will do to them if they answer the door. He takes them to the beach.

Thanks to his excellent small-army management skills, I used to try to sneak away on occasion to work on writing projects and other creative endeavors. I imagined that I could get more done if I didn't have a baby in my arms and a multitude of other creatures dancing around my feet. It makes sense, no? And yet, no matter where in the world I settled down with my laptop, my brain would shut down, or go on vacation, or do anything, it seemed, other than what I wanted it to do, which was to help me put words on the page.

After attempting to write in solitude in a number of different locations (including two hotels, three restaurants, and that cute little pie shop down the road) on a shockingly high number of occasions without any improvement in word count, I gave up.

I packed up my bags, came home, grabbed a baby, sat down with my laptop, and began to write. And write. And write some more. It was as if having a little one on my knee was the key that unlocked my ability to produce content. Which I thought was really, really weird.

Usually when something really, really weird happens to me, it's because God is trying to tell me something. So I asked him. "Hey, God," I said. "What's up? Why won't you let me write in peace while sipping my cafe mocha with half the chocolate and extra whipped cream?"

To which he immediately replied, "So that you will know, my girl, that the privilege of creating art is not reserved for those with hours of free time on their hands. Art is for everyone," he said. "You don't need an artists' retreat or a quiet cafe. You can create things of beauty whenever and wherever you find yourself in life." (You should know that I did gently mention to him that though I might not technically *need* to go to a writing cabin in the woods, I was not opposed to it.)

FOLLOW YOUR FEARS

Where I found myself at that moment in time was knee deep in family life. Growing babies and raising babies, feeding babies and kissing babies. I had piles of laundry up to my ears and a dishwasher that never got a break. I had a to-do list a mile long and, as God had picked up on, was not entirely sure that I should be chasing after artistic pursuits at all.

As ironic as it sounds, by shutting down the right side of my brain every time I left the house, God was telling me that family life and creative life were not incompatible and were, in actual fact, symbiotic.

This is not to say that writing in cafes is a bad thing or somehow an offense against the duties of motherhood. But God knew that I needed to behold just how harmonious the relationship between the two can be. Bringing forth new life, nurturing that life, and producing art — it all emanates from the same creative well. God wanted to show me that there weren't barriers to entry. He wanted me to see that he'd flung open the gates and all were welcome to drink from the well and then go forth and cover the world with bright splashes of paint, mellifluous song, and soul-stirring prose.

But, I asked God, what if my splashes of paint aren't so bright, my song not mellifluous, and my words not prose-ish in the least? What if my art is terrible? What if people laugh? What if they gather around large tables and talk about how very cringe-worthy my art is?

"Yes, well, people do and may," he said, "so, what if?"

God then reminded me of an episode of Dr. Phil that I'd seen a few years earlier during what must have been (we can only hope) either a sleep-deprived temporary lapse in judgment or God showing off and demonstrating that he can work through anyone, no matter how many odd interventions they've facilitated.

Dr. Phil said to follow your fears to their logical conclusion. What is the very worst that could happen? Maybe they will laugh, and maybe they will insult you, and maybe you will cry a little. You'll probably feel embarrassed for a while and want to hide away for a time, but guess what happens next? You will curl yourself into your husband's arms and let your little ones call you "pretty mama." He will remind you that you are the treasure of his heart, and they will pick flowers for you and tell you startling long stories about the dreams they dreamt the night before. After a time, you'll brush yourself off and get back to the business of living.

Rudyard Kipling once said, "Of all the liars in the world, sometimes the worst are our own fears."

My fears have this very bad habit of telling me all sorts of ludicrous stories about all sorts of terrible fates that might befall me, and rarely do I question them.

"So I'm going to produce the worst piece of art ever created? So bad that it will be hung in the Louvre so that people can marvel at what a gruesome thing it is that I've produced? A sort of cautionary tale for the masses? And then I will die a long, drawn-out, torturous death from the shame of it all? You don't say."

One day it occurred to me that maybe there was another way. Maybe instead of giving my fears carte blanche to manage my anxiety levels, I should stop for a moment and examine them. Turn them over in my hands for a bit, peer into all their dark corners, and then, instead of taking them at face value, laugh at all their silly, melodramatic ways. Because they *are* often very silly and melodramatic.

LOVE THE BOMB

But then Stephen Colbert had an even crazier idea. What if, he suggested in a 2015 interview with *GQ*, we could learn, in some small way, to love our fears? Wouldn't that be marvelous?

> "Our first night professionally onstage," he said, the longtime Second City director Jeff Michalski told them that the most important

lesson he could pass on to them was this: "You have to learn to love the bomb."

"It took me a long time to really understand what that meant," Colbert said. "It wasn't 'Don't worry, you'll get it next time.' It wasn't 'Laugh it off.'"

"No, it means what it says. You gotta learn to love when you're failing…. The embracing of that, the discomfort of failing in front of an audience, leads you to penetrate through the fear that blinds you. Fear is the mind killer."

He said he trained himself, not just onstage but every day in life, even in his dream states, to steer toward fear rather than away from it. "I like to do things that are publicly embarrassing," he said, "to feel the embarrassment touch me and sink into me and then be gone. I like getting on elevators and singing too loudly in that small space. The feeling you feel is almost like a vapor. The discomfort and the wishing that it would end that comes around you. I would do things like that and just breathe it in."

He stopped and took in a deep yogic breath, then slowly shook his head. "Nope, can't kill me. This thing can't kill me."

After reading that interview, I realized that I wanted to get to a place where I didn't just grit my teeth and force myself to keep moving forward in spite of my fears but, like Colbert, I wanted to "learn to love the bomb." I was pretty sure that was where I would find the greatest level of freedom.

His interview also made me think of the often repeated question, What would you do if you had no fear? Or if you could not fail? And what things in life are worth doing, whether you succeed or not?

That's always been a bit of a tricky question for me. I think one of the things that has always stopped me from truly leaning into my fears is that I'm not always sure whether my dreams line up well with God's plan for my life. I might be willing to take a leap of faith if I was sure that God wanted me to leap. But I wasn't sure, so for a long time I was unwilling to take a step in any direction.

Everyone kept telling me to discern God's will to the best of my abilities and then jump. God would catch me if I were to fall, they told me.

"But what if I mis-discern," I replied, "and jump off the wrong cliff? What if he's waiting for me on the north side of the mountain and I recklessly leap to the south?"

"Hallie," they said, "don't you know that God will catch you even if you jump off the wrong cliff? He is everywhere — North, East, South, and West. Ever waiting to catch you when you fall. Which you will, by the way."

It took me a long time to understand this. Even longer to believe it. I nodded my head, so as not to offend, but secretly, deep down inside, I suspected that God would only have my back if I perfectly followed the path he had set out before me and got an A+ on all of my discernment tests. Knowing that I'm more of a C student in this area, I figured that I would probably head in the wrong life direction, stumble over a crack in the pavement, and find myself splayed on the pavement.

Sure, maybe God would eventually come along and help me back up, but boy, would he be mad. He'd probably make me wait a very long time, too, in the hopes that my suffering might inspire me to bring my grade up a notch or two. No, better to stand perfectly still. Right smack dab in the middle of the path I was already on.

But that's not the way of God. That's merely the way I pictured God behaving when I viewed him through a lens of fear. When my small mischievous boy climbs to the top of the jungle gym, pretends to be a fighter pilot, jumps from his fiery plane without a parachute, and ends up battered and bruised in the dirt, do I sit back and think: better let him stay there for a while so he learns his lesson? Of course not. I jump up and run to his side.

How silly of me to not understand that God, whose love for me is vastly more pure and passionate than even my love for my own children, will do the same.

Yes, God wants me to discern his will to the best of my abilities. But not because he's a control freak. Rather, because he loves and wants only the best for me. If I misdiscern and get it wrong, as I often do, he's not going be vindictive. Instead he will take me by the hand and say, "Let's give it another go. What do you say, my girl?"

Recently a friend of mine had a big decision to make. She, who had not held a traditional job since before she became a mother, had been offered an exciting career opportunity. One that would allow her to tap into her creativity and help others, but would mean big changes for her family. She was scared of making the wrong decision. Finally, after praying about it for a long time without receiving the clarity she sought, her husband sat her down and told her to go for it. He figured that the worst that could happen would be that she'd get a few months in, discover that she'd made the wrong call, and would have to quit.

I love his approach. In a nutshell, it says: don't blow your fears out of proportion. Yes, you might make the wrong call, and yes, there might be some collateral damage. But what's life without a little risk? You jump, you fall, you get back up, and if you're lucky, you learn a little something about yourself in the process.

When we stay wrapped up inside a cocoon with a safety net securely fastened beneath us, we miss out on so much that life has to offer and a great many lessons that God wants to teach us. We say no to opportunities to learn how to better trust God, refuse to allow him to care for us, take a pass on marvelous adventures, and never get the chance to discover all of the breathtaking things that might make us come alive inside. We choose instead to draw closed the curtains and learn to tamp down the longing inside that begs for us to go outside and explore.

What a tragedy.

SET THE WORLD ON FIRE

But still, I've often wondered, is it prudent for me, with all the responsibilities I have on my plate, to carve out time for creative pursuits? Even considering all of the above, is it not maybe a little selfish? A bit self-indulgent?

A saint thinks not. In his *Letter to Artists*, Pope St. John Paul II wrote:

> In order to communicate the message entrusted to her by Christ, the Church needs art. Art must make perceptible, and as far as possible attractive, the world of the spirit, of the invisible, of God. It must therefore translate into meaningful terms that which is in itself ineffable. Art has a unique capacity to take one or other facet of the message and translate it into colors, shapes, and sounds which nourish the

intuition of those who look or listen. It does so without emptying the message itself of its transcendent value and its aura of mystery.

When God created the world, he dreamed big creative dreams. He dreamt of fanciful frogs with funny legs and of twinkles in babies' eyes. He imagined the sound of rain and the crashing of waves on rocks and countless tiny grains of sand. He envisioned cantaloupes and cocoa beans, crunchy carrots and funny treelike stalks of broccoli. He created it all and then handed it over to us to study and savor.

He said, "Here, have this, and do something wonderful with it. Paint with the pigment of plants and bake with their spices. Make music from the reeds and rocks and string words together with smudges of carbon. Use it all, my little ones, to light up the eyes of your children, bring joy to the sorrowful, and entice the world with the hint of heaven."

And so, you and I, we must. It is part of our purpose. God himself is the one who lit the creative spark inside each of us, and it is the Holy Spirit who keeps it ablaze. Now we must take that flame, and in the words of St. Catherine of Siena, set the world on fire.

What are we waiting for?

CHAPTER FOUR

Home

**My entire life can be described in one sentence:
It didn't go as planned, and that's okay.**
~ Rachel Wolchin

I went through a season not too long ago when I thought I wanted adventure. I was about a decade into marriage and eight years into motherhood, and I felt stuck. Stuck being not quite as good a mother as I'd hoped I'd be. Stuck being not quite as loving a wife as I'd planned. Stuck without the Southern Living-style home I'd aspired to create. Stuck on a spiritual plateau. Stuck buying clothes in ever-increasing sizes. Stuck.

I've always had a touch of wanderlust, and somehow I believed that if I just uprooted my family and moved us to a new spot, I'd become unstuck. In my family, we call this "magical thinking," but at the time it all seemed perfectly reasonable to me.

I started to pray to God, asking him to give us the fresh start I craved. Soon after, a work opportunity presented itself in an entirely new-to-us area of the country. Dan was amenable, if not nearly as desperate for change as I, and off we went, driving almost directly north to a place so different from our beloved South that a scriptwriter couldn't have created a more dramatic contrast.

As we entered the city, my heart sank. It was nothing like I had imagined. In fact, it was the opposite of everything I had hoped for. Which is not to say that this city-that-will-remain-unnamed is not a perfectly lovely city inhabited by perfectly lovely people who would never dream of leaving. It just wasn't for me.

Plenty of great adventures can be had in a place that feels a little foreign and ill fitting. You can savor hiking along snow-covered peaks but not want to live on them. You can feel close to God as you lie underneath a huge star-laden desert sky but still not want to stay there forever. You can have the time of your life (I would imagine) sailing from continent to continent without actually longing to live on a boat forever. The problem wasn't the city itself, the problem was that I didn't know when, or if, I'd ever get to leave. That's when it hit me — it wasn't adventure I yearned for, it was home.

I longed for the kind of home where your roots go down so deep that it's impossible to dig them up. The kind of home that welcomes children back from college and lets them lay their burdens down in the same room where they were rocked as infants. The kind of home where you can envision your grandchildren gathered around your giant farmhouse table even before spouses have been found or aisles walked. And the kind of home where, forgive me for being morbid, you invest in a family burial plot underneath a huge, shady oak tree.

That desire is what had been at the heart of my restlessness, and this new place we'd relocated to, surely a nurturing home to many, was not home to me, and I knew it in an instant. That night I lay on top of a mattress in our new blue bedroom and tried to hold back tears. Dan had done this, at least in part, for me, and I'd made a terrible mistake and didn't know how I was going to tell him. My children would surely be forever damaged by this misstep. I was a terrible wife, a horrible discerner of God's will, and should probably be sent away to a cave so that the rest of humanity could be protected from my life-ruining ways. (It is possible that the fifteen-hour drive had left me a little emotional.)

FIX IT, FIX IT, FIX IT

Over the next few days, anxiety grabbed hold of me, twisting my stomach into knots as I tried not to fixate on the hopelessness of our situation. It wasn't that I couldn't endure, and possibly even enjoy, this place for a time; it was the not knowing when we could leave or how my mistake would be fixed.

Uprooting your family is expensive, and new jobs aren't thick on the ground, so it was clear that if we had any hope of moving anytime soon, God was going to have to get involved. I began to chant a mantra that sounded something like this: "Fix it, fix it, fix it. Sweet, merciful Lord, please fix it. Fix it, fix it, fix it. Have you fixed it yet? Fix it, fix it, fix it. Oh, and God? Here's exactly how I think you should fix it."

How did I think he should fix it? In a flash of divine inspiration, he should show me exactly where we should put down roots; give Dan a job that used his gifts, left him feeling fulfilled, and provided us with just enough income to meet our basic needs; find us a beautiful, but modest, home on a quiet street with a big backyard for our kids to frolic in while I baked and listened to Madeleine Peyroux; introduce us to a supportive community of friends; and lead us to a parish where we would worship for the rest of our lives. That was all. Not so much really, and certainly a reasonable request to make of a God for whom all things are possible.

But the months passed without a response (unless you consider a silent "no" to be a response, which I did not at the time). Half of me wanted to lash out at God for withholding the assistance and consolation we so desperately needed, but the other half of me felt like maybe this was exactly what I deserved for my reckless impulsivity.

Day after day I pleaded with God to lead us out of this desert. I pestered him, I delivered increasingly detailed plans for how exactly he could save us, and I told him exactly what I thought of his stubborn silence. The truth was that I was irritated. What would it cost him to help me right my wrong and lead us to greener pastures? Nothing, of course, but what he could see that I could not was that there would be a cost, a cost that would ultimately be at *my* expense.

I heard a story about a priest who was known for his efficacious prayers. It was said that God granted almost everything for which he prayed. Funds for a new chapel? An unexpected generous check would be waiting for him in the mail the very next day. Support for a new ministry? It would be thriving by the end of the season. And so on.

This baffled me for years. Why was God so eager to answer his prayers and not mine? The only thing I could come up with was that he had that faith of a mustard seed that I obviously lacked. I tried to summon a similar level of faith by preemptively thanking God for granting me all the gifts I begged him for, but I ended up sounding like a presumptuous impostor who over-emoted. For months this question ate away at me until one day, quite by accident (unless you consider that just maybe God had a hand in it), I heard the second half of the story.

The piece I'd been missing, and the answer to all my questions, was that before this holy priest fell to his knees and pleaded with God, he asked God to reveal his will. What was God asking of him? What great adventures did he want this good priest to embark upon? What seemingly impossible tasks was he asking him to undertake? And which small, humble jobs did he need done on that day? Only when he was confident that he had heard the still, small voice of God clearly did he begin to pray for the tools he would need to complete these assignments. He sought God's will first, and then prayed for providence, peace, and patience. That was his secret.

SURRENDER

Inspired by this man, I decided to attempt a shift away from a My Will Be Done mentality to more of a Thy Will Be Done approach. I won't lie, it wasn't easy. Everything in me — all of my fear, pride, and impatience — recoiled at the idea of ceding control to a God who was known for asking his followers to take what appeared to be terribly ill-conceived leaps of faith. But with what little courage I could muster, I tried.

What do you want from me, God? And can it maybe not be too painful? At least for this first experiment, can you please go easy on me, O Lord?

His response was simple. "Be still and know that I am God." Relax. Breathe. Trust. Wait. Stop fighting and scheming and resisting. Couldn't I see how miserable I was making myself? Didn't I know that it was God who allowed my family to move to this foreign land and reside for a time? Could I not trust that he would see me through this trial? And at the heart of it all: "Be at peace."

I started to pray. I prayed for peace. I prayed for the ability to surrender. I prayed that amidst all of my fears, I would be able to trust in him and his plan for our life.

God had felt distant for many months, and a subtle darkness had cast its shadow over everything I'd encountered. Colors seemed muted, my children's laughter was a little less soul stirring, my husband's touch not quite so compelling, my passions somewhat less invigorating, and a slight but persistent sadness clung to my shoulders.

As soon as I started to pray for peace, all of that darkness began to dissipate. As God has been known to do, he parted the clouds and poured in his light. Suddenly I couldn't get enough of good music and rich food, the caress of my husband, and the giggles of my children. I imagine there was even a rainbow in there somewhere, too.

A few weeks later, Dan came to me and, knowing what a difficult time I'd been having, reassured me that he was doing everything he could to find a new home for us. I remember being surprised to find that I no longer felt in any hurry to depart. Though I knew this wasn't where we were meant to stay forever, I'd begun to enjoy our time in this place. We found a parish that we absolutely loved, I discovered a nearby state park that offered the kids and me endless hours of exploration, and suddenly I found all of the strange quirks of the city fascinating rather than irritating. Though I'd believed it impossible, I found that I was at peace.

I don't believe it bothers God one bit when we go to him with our sky-high pile of silly (and not so silly) very specific requests. I imagine he is every bit as tickled by our pleas as Dan is when our young son, Charlie, requests, "Just one more lollipop, peas, Daddy?" But if we are seeking peace, perhaps sometimes — to whatever degree our scared, stubborn selves can stand it — we should admit that maybe there are some things that we can't see and others still that we don't understand.

And maybe we should occasionally ask instead to know what God would have us pray for and do rather than clinging madly to our own vision of what the future should hold. I'm beginning to think that that is where the peace that surpasses human understanding lies.

Even with my newfound contentment in hand, I still longed to find the place where we would put down roots. God hadn't changed the desires of my heart; instead he'd given me peace while I waited for them to be fulfilled. Dan and I knew we wanted to land somewhere in the Southeast and had narrowed our list of possible areas to three — Asheville, North Carolina; Nashville, Tennessee; and Charleston, South Carolina, none of which I'd ever visited. While Dan kept the home fires burning, I set off on a solo road trip to visit these towns and see if I could find the next piece of land we were meant to inhabit.

I hit Asheville first, and while I absolutely loved it and have visited it several times since, I knew that it wasn't the place I'd been seeking. So I continued my journey out of the mountains and down toward the sea.

When I arrived in Charleston, I pulled off of the interstate onto Meeting Street and made my way over to King Street. Before I'd even had a chance to park the car, I was on the phone with Dan telling him that I'd found it. I was home. I could list all of the things I immediately loved about the city, but none of those things were the reason I told Dan that I wanted to live in this place. It was more of a sense that I had asked God for a home and now he was revealing it to me by filling my soul with joy and a very deep love for this land.

In a sudden and clearly God-arranged turn of events, a few days after I returned home, Dan flew down to Charleston to interview for a job. He had stumbled upon the job listing purely by accident and had submitted his resume online and on a whim a week earlier. Before he'd left, we had discussed what kind of salary we would need to support our family. We came up with a very specific number and noted that moving costs would also have to be included since we had nothing in savings.

As he was driving to the airport to catch his flight back that afternoon, he called me. I'd braced myself for weeks of waiting for a verdict, but he had news to share with me already. He'd been offered the job on the spot, with a salary that was, down to the penny, the exact amount we'd determined we would need, plus moving costs. He told me to start packing.

I walked out onto our back porch, sat down on the stairs, and offered a prayer of thanksgiving to the God who, in the end, had given me everything I'd desired — a year of adventure, an important lesson in seeking his will and learning to surrender, the peace that follows, and now, at last, a new home.

CHAPTER FIVE

Blue Lines

**There is no terror in the bang,
only in the anticipation of it.**

~ Alfred Hitchcock

"If this were a blind study, I'd guess I was looking at the bloodwork of a fifty-year-old woman in menopause."

My endocrinologist put down my lab results, looked up at me from the other side of her huge paper-strewn mahogany desk, and smiled.

"So, since you're clearly not fifty, and I'm guessing not in menopause, my diagnosis is that your hormonal system just got a little out of whack from the stress of the wedding and now needs some time to get its act together and reboot. Nothing to worry about."

I looked back at her incredulously. For no apparent reason at the age of twenty-two my hormone levels had plummeted, leaving me, from what everyone could tell, essentially (if supposedly temporarily) infertile. Nothing to worry about?

What she didn't know, couldn't have known, was that I hadn't been under any added stress lately.

Dan and I had been married in a small Spanish-style church only a few months earlier. I walked down the aisle as the sun set, accompanied by my father and the strains of

Pachelbel's Canon. Candles lit the sanctuary, and the scent of gardenias filled the pews. It was a small wedding, thrown together quickly so that my dying grandfather could be with us, but in the end its simplicity is what I loved most about it.

I loved that our programs were homemade and that our cream cheese and pecan-filled butter wedding cake was made by the old woman down the road who covered it with polka dots made of fondant. I adored our reception site, the twinkling light-laden courtyard of a downtown restaurant. The soundtrack of our reception was a collection of three CDs filled with songs that were meaningful to Dan and me. Even the signs that directed the kids to the virgin strawberry daiquiri machine and the adults to the not-so-virgin margarita machine were handcrafted by my (far more artistic) better half. And though our wedding took place less than a month after the September 11 terrorist attacks, somehow everyone we wanted to share our wedding day with found a way to be there. It was everything I could have wanted and more, and the months that had followed had brought only more happiness.

So, no. Unless I was in some sort of extreme denial, what was happening to my body was not the result of stress. I stood and turned to leave. Because what do you say when you're standing in your endocrinologist's office facing her Harvard degrees and her twenty-plus years of experience, and she is insisting that you're suffering from an everyday, if not a bit temperamental, bout of stress despite all of your protestations?

You smile, thank her, and make plans to have a one-on-one in-depth conversation with Google.

It didn't take long for Dr. Google to render a diagnosis: premature ovarian failure. Odds of conception over the remainder of my lifetime: 5–10 percent. Odds of Hallie having a complete nervous breakdown as a result of said determination: 100 percent.

As a teenager I'd been emphatic that I had no desire to have children. At the time, I'm sure everybody but me understood that I was taking some ridiculous stand against heaven knows what, but I believed myself even if no one else did. I was genuinely surprised when, after falling in love with Dan, I discovered a hunger for children inside of me that felt at once both utterly surprising and perfectly natural. I craved motherhood, could feel the weight of a newborn heavy in my empty arms. The possibility that I might never be able to bear children terrified me.

I'd converted not a year earlier, and I suddenly realized that handing your life over to God isn't a guarantee that everything will go smoothly. I knew that, in theory. I'd seen Christians suffer and knew martyrs had died, but up until this point I'd carried around an overly romanticized notion of what the Christian life would feel like. I believed, naively, that God's grace was like a strong prescription painkiller. Sure, you would need to be cut open so that all of the ugly stuff inside you could be removed, so that you could be made new, but surely grace would come along and somehow allow you to smile through the agony. In fact, it would somehow largely protect you from truly experiencing it at all. I didn't yet know that the agony is an essential part of being made new.

SEARCHING FOR A FORECAST

I heard the front door open and quickly turned off my computer. I found Dan crouched down in front of our CD player searching, as he always did upon returning home, for the perfect song to start off the evening.

"Hey, sweetie. How did your day go? What did the doctor say?" he asked.

"She said I'll be fine. That my system just needs time to reboot."

The Housemartin's hit song *Happy Hour* began to play as I began to sob.

"Wait. What's going on? Why are you crying?" Dan rushed to my side.

"I'm never ... going ... to ... have children." My worst fear came pouring out of me in fits and bursts, as water does from a thawing frozen pipe.

"But you just said that the doctor said you're going to be fine," Dan said, looking at me quizzically.

"She was wrong," I said.

"She was wrong? How do you know?"

"Because she says I'm stressed out, and I'm not. She said stress caused this, but I'm not stressed! I mean, I am now, but I wasn't before! I tried to tell her, but she wouldn't listen. Anyway, I did a little research of my own this afternoon, and I think I have premature ovarian failure."

Dan was silent. I think he knew that he would one day look back upon this moment as his first true test as a married man.

"This research you did ... what sources did you use? Who did you talk to?"

"The Internet. I've been reading articles about this all afternoon."

"And you feel like the Internet knows better than your endocrinologist?" he asked gently.

"No! I think *I* know better than my endocrinologist! I know whether I've been under stress, and I know what my symptoms feel like!"

Dan rubbed my back and was silent for a moment.

"You know," he said, "whatever happens, we're going to be fine. We have each other, we have God, and he has a plan for our family."

"Well, his plan sucks if it means that I don't get to be a mother."

Dan laughed. "Yeah, it often feels that way."

"It doesn't just feel that way. It is that way." I burst into tears. "You should have married someone else. We haven't even been married a year, and I'm already a failure of a wife."

He kissed my head and hushed me. Silently grabbing me by the hand, he put me in the car and drove to the frozen custard stand down the road. Even then, without the benefit of years of marital experience, he knew that when words fail, frozen custard is a solid Plan B.

Months passed without a change in my symptoms, my gestational status, or my mood. I was angry with God. So deeply angry. And scared. The creating of family seemed to me to be such a pure desire. I possessed a great many less pure aspirations and could kind of (albeit begrudgingly) accept his negative verdict on those issues, but his "no" to my request for children seemed capricious and heartless. The decision to deny Dan fatherhood, even crueler still. Dan, with his childlike spirit and playful demeanor, was made to raise children. It was in standing next to him that I was first able to envision myself as a mother.

One of the things that first drew me to Catholicism was its emphasis on and celebration of the family, and I wanted so desperately to participate in that goodness within the walls of my own home. I'd worked in a baby goods store for a time before I was married and had purchased a painting created by a local artist of five little girls standing in the rain. In their hands they held rainbow-colored umbrellas and on their feet were matching rain boots. It was now tucked in the back of my closet, waiting to be hung in a nursery. Every time I spotted its rich colors peeking out from behind my coats, a lump formed in my throat. Its presence was a constant reminder of just how much I yearned to wipe runny noses, rock sleepy babies, and feed my child from my breast. Day after day, I cursed my defective body with each intake and exhalation of breath.

There were moments when I could concede that perhaps my doctor was right and I was wrong, but even those moments were painful for the not knowing, the lack of certainty. If this were merely a temporary departure from my years of healthy fertility, when would it end? I alternated between hope and despair, moved in and out of shadow and light.

Since I clearly couldn't have a baby now, I begged God for a forecast. I thought I could suffer through anything if I knew when the pain would end. The idea that it might never end was an eventuality that, ironically, left me curled in the fetal position on my bed for days on end. (In the fetal position with ice cream in hand and reality TV on the screen in front me, but in the fetal position, nonetheless.)

FLUNKING THE TEST

Dan, on the other hand, seemed to be perfectly at peace. This would prove to be the first of a series of life challenges in which he displayed an innate ability to trust in God that left me baffled. The harder we were asked to stretch, the deeper Dan bent to align his will with God's. At times I found this inspiring, at other times infuriating. I couldn't decide whether I thought Dan was significantly holier than I or significantly more foolish, and both conclusions had the potential to irritate me when I was in the depths of struggle.

Deep down inside, though, I knew that such feelings were the result of my own insecurities and fears rearing their ugly heads. In truth, I couldn't have asked for a more supportive husband. He was the calm, quiet rock amidst my raging storm. He never grew impatient with me as I cried, never failed to drive me down to the frozen custard shop when all else failed, and never neglected to wrap his arms around me, reassure me of his love, and tell me that everything was going to be fine.

We just had to trust, he said.

Trusting in someone other than myself has never come easy for me. I am not a "Jesus, take the wheel" kind of gal. I'm more of a "Jesus, you can hop into my passenger seat as long as you promise not to be a backseat driver" kind of gal. The thing about physical ailments, though, is that you can't will yourself back to health. You can visit doctors, take medication, and generally become a healthier person, but when those things fail, as I believed they were for me, the only path left to you is to humbly ask God for assistance.

For someone who was new to the humility game (and not terribly good at it) this was an emotional experience. I bristled at the idea that in turning to God and asking him for help I was, in essence, accepting that the help he delivered might not look the way I'd hoped it would or arrive on my timeline.

Our first Christmas as a married couple had come and gone, and our second was looming. I continued to detect absolutely no improvement in my hormonal situation, which, to me, seemed to confirm that Dr. Google was a whole lot smarter than my endocrinologist. One might think that over the course of fourteen months I'd grown a little more accepting of God's apparent plan for my life, but the opposite was true. I grew more anxious and resentful with each passing month. I felt utterly abandoned by God and wanted to know why just months after turning my life over to him, he was punishing me so. Was he angry with me for past sins? Had I proved to be a disappointment to him? Did he simply not care all that much about me?

He was silent on these issues, and it was the silence that ate away at me the most. Where was the consolation I'd been told would be present during times of strife? Where were the quiet whispers that told me I was not alone and exhorted me to be at peace? Why could I not feel deep down inside, the way Dan did, that everything would be fine? I searched for answers but over and over again came up empty.

I knew that my faith was immature, and I understood that becoming a saint, and behaving in a saintly fashion, was a lifelong process. But given all of this, why send such a painful test my way so early on in my journey? It seemed to me that God had made a mistake and had sent me a Spiritual Life AP test instead of the Spiritual Life 101 test that I was supposed to be taking.

HOPE

A few months into our struggle to conceive, something, or rather Someone, told me to write to Mother Angelica, the nun who founded the EWTN television network, asking for prayers. I had heard story after story about her efficacious prayers, so being willing to try anything I pulled out my cream-colored linen stationery and put pen to paper.

I had, over the course of the last year, convinced myself that I would never get pregnant. No longer did I have any faith in my endocrinologist. At this point I'd even given up hope in Dr. Google's 5–10 percent chance of conception. I was as sterile as sterile could be. That I knew with a stubborn certainty. Despite my fatalistic attitude, though, I scrawled words upon the page until my fingers ached and my eyes swam. I poured out my heart to Mother as I shared the details of my desire for children, my physical state, and my spiritual struggles. I even went so far as to address it, put a stamp on it, and slip it into the mailbox. For someone who is terrible at producing snail mail, this was no small thing. But mail it I did, and then I promptly forgot all about it.

On the kind of cold, rainy January day that makes you crave cocoa and cozy blankets and curling up on couches, the mail slot on our front door squeaked open, and I heard our daily allotment of mail drop to the floor. I kneeled on our living room floor and collected the scattered envelopes. At the very bottom was a slightly soggy envelope, return address: Our Lady of the Angels Monastery. One of Mother Angelica's nuns had replied. The card was short but sweet and informed us that not only were their prayers with us but that they had arranged to have a Mass offered for our intentions.

Something released in my chest, and the heart that I had allowed to slowly harden over the past few months cracked open. A floodgate of tears came pouring out. Though I didn't know her personally, and had met her briefly only once, Mother Angelica meant a lot to me. I'd spent hour upon hour watching her on EWTN as she answered questions about the faith, doled out her no nonsense but always affectionate advice, and comforted the downtrodden and heartbroken sinners of the world. Just the idea that she and her Sisters were praying for me filled me with hope, something that I'd been sorely in need of.

THE WRECKAGE OF THE FUTURE

I was also sorely in need of perspective. A few years ago, my friend Cate was sharing a laundry list of her fears with a friend of hers when her friend stopped her.

"You've got to stop living in the wreckage of the future, Cate. None of these things you're afraid of have actually happened, you know."

The moment Cate shared this story with me, I knew that I'd been doing the same thing. I'd taken up residence in a place in which all of my worst nightmares had come true. The fact that this was an imaginary place did not stop me from putting up a white picket fence, planting a lovely row of tulips, and spending an inordinate amount of time on my front porch bemoaning my terrible lot in life.

The more I talk with others about anxiety, the more I see that Cate and I are not the only ones who struggle with the temptation to live in dread of things that have not and may never play out. Even Mark Twain feels our pain. I knew I'd found a kindred spirit when a friend sent me this quote: "I've lived through some terrible things in my life, some of which actually happened."

During this time in my life, when everything in me craved, but was denied, a child of my own, life was good. Dan and I were madly in love and had few responsibilities and more freedom than two people knew what to do with. God was pouring so much goodness into our life. But because I was so consumed with fear, so moved-in to the wreckage of the future, I couldn't appreciate it the way I should have. I regret that. I regret that I wasn't able to summon enough trust to savor every bit of goodness that God wanted to give me in that present moment. I wonder sometimes how much I missed.

During a recent Q&A session following a talk I'd given at a parish, a young woman asked me what one piece of advice I, a married woman with children, could give to her, a single woman. "Enjoy your life just as it is today," I said after thinking about it for a few seconds. "Don't worry about all of the things God has not yet given you and don't fret about the future. Savor the deliciousness of this moment. You only get to live today once. Don't let it pass you by."

****

In early February, shortly after I received the letter from Mother Angelica and her nuns, I began to suspect that I might be pregnant. I'd gotten my hopes up so many times over the course of the past year only to have them dashed, though, so I pushed my giant box of pregnancy tests to the back of the closet and tried not to think about it.

Later that week, Dan and I attended morning Mass to celebrate the Feast of St. Blaise, the day on which Catholics practice the ancient tradition of getting our throats blessed. I had always loved those external symbols of spiritual realities and, though I hadn't revealed my suspicions to Dan, I was secretly planning on gathering strength from them and then heading home to take a pregnancy test.

I closed my eyes as the priest crossed candles over my throat and uttered the words of blessing: "Through the intercession of St. Blaise, bishop and martyr, may God deliver you from every disease of the throat and from every other illness: In the name of the Father, and of the Son, and of the Holy Spirit."

I felt encouraged, and yet an agitation stayed with me. I walked back to the pew, impatiently watching the rays of dawn's sunlight as inch by inch they climbed up the stained glass windows.

The moment the Mass ended I hurried up the aisle and headed for the exit.

"Do you want to grab breakfast before I head into work, sweetheart?" Dan asked.

"No, I just want to go home." I replied quickly.

"Okay. Is everything alright?"

"Yes, but I want to go home." I bowed my head as we walked down the steps of St. Mary's to avoid being caught up in one of those seemingly endless post-Mass parking lot conversations and hurried to the car.

As soon as Dan unlocked the front door, I made a beeline for the bathroom. Two minutes later, while he was making breakfast, I choked out a scream that sounded vaguely like his name. He ran to the bathroom. There he found me on my knees, tears streaming down my face, with two perfect tiny blue lines cradled in my trembling hands.

Mother Angelica had called, and God had answered.

 Chapter Six

Abraham

**Those who sincerely say "Jesus, I trust in you"
will find comfort
in all their anxieties and fears.**

~ St. John Paul II

After seven years of homeschooling, I did the last thing I ever expected to do and filled out an application to send my three oldest kids to a small private Christian school down the street from us. This decision was almost as unexpected as my decision to homeschool to begin with.

I had never expected to educate my children at home. I had not been homeschooled and was fairly certain that I would be the last person on earth God would call to do so. My friend Kelly didn't share my confidence, though. One day, while we were sitting at Starbucks — in an apparent attempt to demonstrate that she didn't know me at all — Kelly suggested that I consider it.

"Ha. Absolutely not. I am the least patient person on the face of the earth and have absolutely no interest in teaching. I would die, my children would be illiterate, and God would weep."

"I don't know. You keep talking about it. I can't help but wonder if God is trying to get your attention."

She had a point and, especially since she wasn't a homeschooler herself, my attention. Without really even meaning to, I kept bringing the topic up in conversation. I knew it was not for our family, but I was intrigued by the idea and hugely respected people who homeschooled.

"Just think about it. Pray about it. Talk to Dan. You never know what God might have in store for your family."

I honestly didn't want to homeschool my kids. But little by little, I began to pray. My interest had been piqued, so I read countless books on the subject and followed Dan around the house telling him about everything I'd learned. And then, one day, I woke up and I knew. God was calling us to homeschool. No one was more surprised than I. But homeschool we did, and for many years it brought us great joy.

Until it didn't.

HOP TO IT

When my oldest son was eleven, I hit a wall. I was pregnant with my seventh child and learning quickly that pregnancy in the second half of your thirties is vastly different than pregnancy in your twenties (or even early thirties, for that matter). I was burned out on teaching and easily frustrated. My kids picked up on my apathy and irritation and, as kids do, followed my lead. Every lesson was a battle.

I was discussing all of this with my friend Kimberly when she mentioned that she'd recently discovered an amazing new private school and was planning to send a couple of her kids there. She encouraged me to take a tour of the school.

"It sounds wonderful, but we don't have the money to cover tuition."

"Just go look at it. It can't hurt. You never know what God might do."

I am not a person who relishes leaving the house during my third trimester. Especially not to take tours of schools with six kids in tow. But I have learned the hard way that when God prompts me to do something, I should hop to it, and I felt him nudging me now.

We toured the school and were blown away by it. We loved their approach to learning and the kindness that poured out of everyone we met, students and teachers alike. There was something special about this place.

Still, I had my doubts. We couldn't afford it, my kids had never attended a brick-and-mortar school, and God had called us to homeschool. How could I turn my back on that call? It seemed to me that what I really needed was to get my act together and do better.

While we were touring the school, the kids were invited to sit in on a day of classes. As soon as our car pulled out of the parking lot, my three oldest kids started begging me to let them do so. I told them I would think about it and then bought them giant milkshakes in an attempt to distract them and hopefully make them forget about it entirely.

It wasn't that I didn't crave a break. It was that I was scared. Scared of entrusting my kids and their education to someone else, of failing to do God's will because I was weak and undisciplined, and of stretching us even further out of our financial comfort zone. Scared of the unknown.

That night I told Dan about the tour and shared my fears. He had a few doubts of his own but thought it might be wise to at least let the kids try attending the school for a day. As usual, he possessed a supernatural calm about the whole thing. I, on the other hand, continued to fret and begged God to start slamming doors closed left and right so that we could put this silly idea behind us and return to the miserable homeschooling grind. (Yes, I am my own worst enemy.)

Alas, Daniel, Jack, and Sophia toured the school and, if possible, fell even more deeply in love with it. They begged us to let them attend. This, of course, only served to compound my stress because I hated the thought of breaking their hearts, but I continued to have serious reservations. Dan and I told them that we would continue to explore the idea and let them know later that month what we had decided.

FEAR AND THE WHAT IFS

I am a great lover of hyperbole, but it's no exaggeration to say that this was one of the most difficult decisions I have ever had to make. I was utterly spent physically, completely burned out on homeschooling, and had no idea how I was going to continue homeschooling in that state with a mischievous two-year-old and a newborn in my arms. But I was terrified of making this change. For weeks I went back and forth, spending night after sleepless night torturing myself with "what ifs."

One night, unable to sleep yet again, I turned to God and said, "I can't make this decision. I just can't. I need you to tell me what to do." Not twelve hours later I was on the phone with Dan when he casually said, "Next year when the kids are in school…."

"What do you mean? When the kids are in school? Are we sending the kids to school? When did we decide this?"

"Oh. Did we not talk about this? I've decided that we should send them. Maybe it will only be for a year, but you have got to have a break. I want you to have a break, sweetheart."

It hasn't been my way, historically speaking, to let other people make decisions for me, but I knew this was the answer to my prayer. I had asked God for a decision, and through Dan he had given me one.

And yet, even after the decision had been made, I continued to worry. What if people were mean to them? What if going to school was too much of a culture shock? What if they couldn't keep up academically? What if we had made the wrong decision and weren't doing God's will? The sleepless nights continued.

Our son, Max, was born right in the middle of this discernment process. Shortly after his birth Dan took him to the chapel at our parish and consecrated him. He held Max in his arms and, on his knees, thanked God for the gift of our child and offered our son back to him. While it was more of a symbolic gesture than an Abrahamic one, it was sincere. He had done the same with all of our other babies, as well.

As I sat in that cool, dimly lit chapel and watched Dan, I suddenly understood in a new and profound way that long before we loved Max, God had loved him. Before he was our child, he was God's. God knew him even before he had knit him in my womb and, though it is a thought that is hard for me to comprehend, he cares for him and his well-being vastly more than I do.

FILLING IN THE CRACKS

It is an honor and a privilege to have been entrusted with caring for these sweet small souls of mine, but at the end of the day God's path and plan for my children does not rely on me being a perfect parent. Their ultimate success in this life and the next is not contingent on my making the right decisions every time or behaving impeccably morning,

noon, and night. His plan to entrust flawed tiny human beings to flawed parents would have been, well, a very flawed
one if that had been his expectation.

When I was a new mother, though, I understood that
even less than I do now. I couldn't articulate it and was not
fully aware of what I was doing, but nevertheless I operated
under the assumption that the fate of my children, body
and soul, rested entirely on my ability to choose the right
brand of diaper. They might become saints if their meals
were wholesome enough, but if I failed to stimulate their in-
tellects adequately, all would be thrown into jeopardy. And
heaven forbid I should lose my temper and snap at them.
How would they ever recover?

Of course, it goes without saying, I hope, that I want
only the best for my little ones. I'd give them the moon if
they asked and I could reach it. But motherhood humbles
you quickly, wasting no time at all in bringing you face to
face with your limitations. That's when you have a choice to
make. Will you continue to exert a death grip on circumstances outside of your control or will you admit that you
are fallen and flawed, desperately in need of a Redeemer,
and learn to let go a little?

I tried the former for a while, making everyone
around me miserable in the process, but finally, begrudgingly, I settled on the latter. My carpet is lucky it doesn't
have a groove carved into it for all the laps from room to
room I've walked as I gaze upon my sleeping children and
ask God to heal the hurt I've caused and compensate for all
the things I've failed to give them.

Because I do hurt and fail them. Every day. I don't
want to, and I fight it with all my might, but I'm impatient
and imperfect and known to get really irritated when they
flood the bathroom. I am learning that the more I allow

God to pour his love into me, the more love I will have to pour back into them, but it's a slow process learning how to receive and give love. So, in the meantime, I pray something along these lines: "Help me to love them better and more. Fill in the cracks that formed when I failed to be careful enough with them. Let their innocent minds remember the happy times more often than they remember the sad. Fill them with your love and grace." And hope that it's enough.

One day, shortly after I'd submitted the school applications, I opened my email inbox and saw waiting for me a letter of acceptance for our children along with the offer of a very generous tuition discount.

I'd love to say that in this turn of events I could see God revealing his will and took comfort in that. To some degree it would be true. I saw God's hand at work and could almost hear him whisper that it's okay to change course. Just because he calls us to something in one breath does not mean that he might not call us to something else in the next. Life is a constant process of discernment with a multitude of twists and turns in the road.

However, when it comes to making decisions that affect my kids, I worry that I've made the wrong decision. And this fear does not easily abate. But I'm learning to be okay with that — I've come to view it as part of the Via Dolorosa of parenting. It's when I stop worrying about such things that I'll be concerned.

The truth is that even if I did everything right, never made a single misstep, and exerted control over their every last movement, I would still end up one day mourning and weeping in the valley of parenting tears. Ultimately, my children will undertake their own unique journey with God, and it won't always be pretty or pleasant. They will be refined by fire over and over again as God forges them into his image and likeness. They will stumble and fall and grow, question and argue and choose, be joyful and sad, and hopefully one day discover the person God means them to be.

This is good and bad news. On one hand, we don't get to control everything. This is painful. But on the other hand, we don't *have* to control everything, and this is liberating. There is great peace to be found in the knowledge that God loves our little ones far more than we ever could. We can't protect our kids from every hurt, but we can, over and over again, offer them back to the one who can heal them.

CHAPTER SEVEN

Edel Soup

**You can't do anything brave if you're wearing
the straight jacket of what will people think.**

~ Brené Brown

For several years during elementary school I attended a performing arts class. It was held in a veterans' hall nestled in a grove of giant oak trees in Northern California. It was the highlight of my week.

One day during class I followed a middle-school–aged girl out into the hallway to get a sip of water from the drinking fountain. I looked up at her, smiled a wide, happy smile, and said hello. I thought she might want to be my friend. She leaned over to get a drink of water, turned to me, and spit it in my face.

I guess not.

I stood stone still as water dripped down my face and onto my shirt. My tear-stung eyes stayed focused on a small spot on the floor, too humiliated to look up and into the eyes of potential witnesses.

I went to a private school when I was young. My school emphasized being kind and loving above almost all else. There were occasional disagreements on the playground, but for the most part everyone was kind and loving and did as they were told. We sang songs about peace and learned about numbers by hearing stories about gnomes and their golden beads. There were lots of rainbows on the wall, and we learned how to be gentle with our plants.

It was very nice, really. I remain staunchly in favor of a sheltered existence for children. The only downside was, I suppose, that I had absolutely no idea how to handle the situation at hand.

I decided that doing nothing at all was probably the safest course of action and shuffled back into the large gathering room. I saw Spit Girl whispering to her band of merry mean girls, watched them giggle, figured they were probably talking about me, and decided to head to the farthest possible corner away from them. I sat down and let my hair fall over my face and past the knees I'd tucked under my chin until it was time to go home.

To this day, I don't know why she did what she did. I was a friendly, if somewhat shy, child and had given her no reason to dislike me. There was, as it turned out, no one around to witness her cruel act, no one she was trying to impress. In retrospect, I think she was probably overwhelmed by some secret pain that she could no longer keep hidden inside and was at the mercy of an anger that demanded to be released. Though older than I, she was still young, and perhaps like a wounded animal, she couldn't help but to lash out at anyone who came near without invitation.

I didn't understand that at the time, though.

What I did understand was that from that day forth it would be far safer for me to keep my eyes downcast and my heart shuttered against the mercurial whims of my fellow human beings. It's hard to spit at someone who's virtually invisible.

Later, in high school, a new friend admitted that she had always found me intimidating. At the time, I thought that was one of the silliest things I'd ever heard. What on earth could have led her to be scared of me? But when I looked down at my all black outfit, considered the way I walked the halls — eyes down with a slight glare on my face as if daring the world to hurt me — I could kind of see why. Inside, I was just a frightened little girl. But to the outside world, yes, I suppose I did look a little intimidating. I'd become, like the girl who had spit in my face, a wounded animal desperate to protect herself from further harm.

And then I met Sara. Sara was a senior and was everything I wasn't — open-hearted, vulnerable, nurturing. She wasn't the prettiest or most popular girl in school and had as many reasons as the rest of us to be self-conscious and afraid, but it didn't appear that she cared. She was warm and bubbly, addressed younger students with terms of endearment, was always ready with a hug and a smile, and spent countless hours listening to our angst-y high school girl woes. She was love and encouragement in a ruthless world inhabited by the insecure.

I wanted to be just like her.

To stop being afraid. To welcome people with a warm smile. To make them feel good about themselves. Loved. Supported. Encouraged.

It would take me over a decade to get anywhere close.

It took years of forcing myself to make eye contact and offer encouragement before I stopped being afraid that my smiles would be met with glares and my warmth with derision. Not until I'd completed hundreds of tiny acts of bravery was I able to let my guard down against the adult equivalent of having water spit in my face. To social butterflies and happy extroverts my words probably ring strange, but I had to work at this very hard and for a long time.

MADNESS

Sometimes I forget that God is always paying attention, but then he goes and does something crazy and I am reminded. He was listening when, as a young girl, I said that one day I'd like to be like Sara with a shoulder ever available to lean on and a smile always at the ready. I imagine he tapped his heavenly pencil for a while as he decided what to do with this small request of mine. Then a few years ago he had an idea.

"I know!" he said. "I'm going to ask Hallie and her friend, Jen, to host a conference for hundreds of women. A conference that has as its sole purpose the encouragement of tired, struggling mothers! Brilliant!" And then he probably patted himself on the back for coming up with such a genius idea.

It should be noted for the record that we tried to argue with him. We told him what an ill-conceived plan this was. "We're introverts!" we said. "With twelve children between the two of us! This is madness, God! Utter insanity!" But he just laughed lovingly and said, "No, no, this is really quite perfect. I'm sure of it." And so we had ourselves a conference. We named her Edel.

A few weeks before the first Edel Gathering, I received an email from one of the attendees. She had thought about it, she said, and wasn't sure she should attend, didn't think she would fit in. She didn't have a dress for the cocktail party and felt uncomfortable in her skin, having recently gained weight while mourning the loss of a child. She was sad, too, for obvious reasons, and afraid she'd put a damper on the festive atmosphere. Could we give her a refund or help her sell her ticket?

I told her that yes, we could, but I hoped she'd reconsider. Though all women were welcome at our event, we planned the gathering with mothers in mind. Most moms don't lead tidy lives. We lead rather messy lives, actually. We welcome children and long for children and we lose children. We are often poor and almost always tired. We are introverts and extroverts, left brained-leaning and right, tall and short, thin and curvy, conservative and liberal, shy and outgoing, happy and sad, all worshipping together to the best of our fallen abilities.

This event we were planning was for all of them. For her.

I told her that I hoped she'd bring her pain and her fears and lay them down at the feet of her sisters in Christ so that we could lift her up. I told her that our event would not be complete without her. I knew I was right. I just didn't know how right I was.

IT IS GOOD, LORD

A couple of nights before the first Edel Gathering I popped a Benadryl and turned out the light at 9 p.m. I had to be up at 4 a.m. to catch a flight to Austin and didn't want to start the weekend sleep-deprived. Hour after painfully long hour passed as I tossed and turned. I counted sheep, prayed Hail Marys, and got increasingly agitated until finally I told God that if he was going to refuse to let me sleep, we might as well be productive.

Was there anything he wanted me to tell the women of Edel during my opening address? Anything he needed them to know? Instantly, seven words popped into my head: "*It is good that you are here.*" Over and over again those words repeated in my head.

"Seriously, God?" I thought. "You want me to tell these women that it is good that they are here? Don't you think that's going to sound a little weird? *Of course* I think it's good that they are here. I was the one who was so nervous that no one would come to this gathering that I made my kids pray for the success of the event!"

But he was insistent.

"It is good that you are here."

I continued to doubt myself (and God) for the next two days. In fact, I'd decided that I was going to cut that part of my talk entirely. But then, as I was walking down the hall at the hotel, a friend pulled me aside and shared a personal story with me. She had suffered a painful tragedy only days before she was scheduled to fly out to Austin to attend the gathering. She was worried that she had made the wrong decision and wasn't sure she should have come. It was the last nudge I needed from God. The Holy Spirit's seven words got a reprieve.

Even though I knew I was meant to speak them, I still felt stupid doing so. After giving my opening address, I walked to the back of the room thinking, "Thanks a lot, God. Do you realize how ridiculous we sounded up there? I knew we should have left that part out."

It is a good thing that our God is a patient and merciful God because as it turned out, you will not be surprised to hear, God knew what he was doing. All throughout the rest of the day, woman after woman approached me to tell me how much they had needed to hear those seven words. Though the details of their stories were unique, the theme running through all of them was the same: they had all experienced some level of anxiety about attending Edel. They had all almost stayed home. But they were all glad they had chosen to come.

Later that day I heard my phone ding and saw that a friend had sent me a picture of a page from a hymnal. She was at the Vigil Mass that many of our guests were attending and wanted me to see the Communion hymn they were singing: *'Tis Good, Lord, to be Here.*

That God of ours, he's a subtle one.

The woman who had emailed me before the conference decided to attend, as well, and, as promised, brought along all of her wounds and her scars. She brought her giant heart and her indomitable spirit, too. Throughout the weekend, she embraced vulnerability, let herself be loved, and loved those around her. She cried freely and laughed with abandon. She told her story. And what a story it was — complete with drama and heartbreak, miracles and happy endings. Many people commented that she ended up being the heart of that year's Edel Gathering.

She could have stayed home. It's scary to step into a room of strangers and say, "Here I am, with all my flaws and fears! Please like me!" Much easier to stay home under a quilt and read, I think. But she summoned her courage and she conquered her fears, and we were all better for it. She taught us how to love with more tenderness and carry our crosses with a little less bitterness, and she showed us what it looks like to be fully and unapologetically the person God created you to be. (She also killed it at karaoke.)

The same is true for all the women who attended. They all had lessons to teach and gifts to share. Without them the event would still have taken place and there would have been many beautiful, fun, and soul-stirring elements, but their unique contributions, their singular brand of themness, would have been missing — or would have lacked a primary ingredient — and though we wouldn't have been able to put our finger on what flavor was missing exactly, we would have all quietly wondered.

THE RISK OF VULNERABILITY

It's easy to think about all of the frightening and disastrous things that might be waiting for us one step beyond our comfort zones, but what about all of the glorious things? What if God is calling us out into the great unknown because he has a gift for us? Or needs for us to share our gifts with someone else? What are we missing when, like my adorable, stubborn two-year-old son, Charlie, we cross our arms in front of us, plant our feet firmly on the ground, jut out our chins, and shake our heads *no*? A great many wondrous things, I bet.

Not that knowing that necessarily makes taking that first step out into the unknown any easier. The world can be a cruel place full of many wounded souls wounding others. It's a fact of life that at some point or another we are going to get hurt.

I recently lost a friend. Not to death, thank God, but to friendship. We had known each for a long time, drifting in and out of ever-changing levels of closeness as life moved through different seasons. Then one day I heard that she was saying unkind things behind my back. We hadn't talked for a while, so I wasn't sure where all of this was coming from and for a while was sure there must have been a mistake. Something must have been lost in translation. But as she stayed silent and then unfriended me on one social media platform after another, it became clear that she really didn't much want to have anything to do with me anymore.

I thought that this should have upset me quite a bit, but strangely I was fine.

I searched my conscience, replayed our recent interactions over in my mind, and couldn't think of a single thing I had done that might have hurt her. I hated that there was discord between us, but ultimately I was at peace.

I imagine she continues to think poorly of me. Once upon a time that would have eaten away at me and stolen my sleep. I would have feared that she was turning others against me and that before I knew it the entire world would despise me. I would have tried to convince her that she was wrong and probably would have ended up apologizing for something I hadn't done. And my poor, poor friends would never have heard the end of it.

The days seem to decrease in length with each passing year. Here in the second half of my thirties I'm struck by how many youthful hours I've wasted worrying about what others thought of me. I wonder what joy and beauty I've missed out on experiencing while I kept my head down, afraid to draw the attention of those who might insult or dislike me. And I think I'm done with all that.

No more.

Instead, I want to cultivate love, savor life, nurture friendships, tell the truth, accept gifts, and share them. I want to sing and dance and make an utter fool of myself if I so choose. I want to be empathetic and authentic, generous and kind. I want to try and fail and fall and try again, laughing, and sometimes crying, through it all. I want to risk and invest and lose and mourn and love again.

I want the fullness of the human experience, and the only way to get it, I'm learning, is to embrace vulnerability. To accept that not everyone is going to like me as much as I might wish they would, which is a scary thing. But what I find even more frightening is the possibility that I might miss out on life entirely because I was afraid of getting hurt.

I have a friend who likes to remind me that most of the time "it's not about you." The email that did not receive a reply? Not about me. The coolness I felt when I saw a friend at the store. Not about me. The invitation that was declined. Also not about me.

"Hallie," he says, "you don't know what's really going on here. This person could have received a devastating diagnosis, be in a fight with her husband, or just be overwhelmed by life so, unless you did something dastardly to her, it's most likely not about you."

For the most part, I know he's right. And it's a good thing to remember. But sometimes it is about you. Or at least directed at you. People may spit on you or decide they don't want to be your friend any longer, and in order to get to a place where we can live life to its fullest, not worrying about what other people think of us, we have to learn to be alright with that.

That I will get hurt is a certainty. So will you. We live in a world full of broken people, and broken people break things. But guess what? That's why we have God. God who is ever-present, and wholly good, and always ready to pick us up, dust us off, and hand us the ticket to our next adventure.

Bon voyage, sweet friends.

CHAPTER EIGHT

Onward

**Love is a festival. Love is joy.
Love is to keep moving forward.**

~ Pope Francis

I used what little energy I had left to put together a handful of peanut butter and jelly sandwiches as I rushed to get dinner on the table before the St. Junipero Serra canonization coverage began.

As far as dinners go, it wasn't going to win me any Parent of the Year awards, but given that I (a) had bronchitis, (b) was on solo parent duty that night, and (c) had included fresh fruit in the dinner lineup, I considered it a victory.

I'd been sick for over three months when Pope Francis came to visit the United States in the fall of 2015. None of my illnesses was life threatening — little more than a series of miserable colds accompanied by a seemingly endless and severe case of bronchitis and one brief but very painful double ear infection that left my hearing impaired for over a month (not the worst symptom a mother of seven has ever experienced, I have to admit) — but the relentlessness of these maladies was exhausting. Just when I'd see the light at the end of one viral tunnel, another would suck me in.

The good news was that my rock bottom coincided nicely with Papa's touchdown on American soil. Due to my inability to do much more than the bare minimum required for survival, I had more freedom than usual to sit and watch him while I nursed my milky sweet newborn.

I'd spent the last twenty-four hours glued to my computer screen as Francis moved from one event to the next, weaving in and out of one crowd after another. I watched with just the slightest touch of jealousy as mothers with newborns as tiny as mine begged Pope Francis's security detail to squire their babies over the barricades, through the air, and into his embrace. Over and over again, I replayed videos of him demanding that his driver stop the car so that he could kiss modern-day lepers.

There were moments when he looked tired. There were even a few times when he seemed mildly annoyed. It was noted by the press that these moments seemed to coincide quite perfectly with the ones in which he was spending time with politicians rather than in the company of his flock. (To such speculation, the Vatican had no comment.) He never once looked overwhelmed, impatient, or stressed, though. Not to me, anyway.

This was remarkable to me. Here was this seventy-eight-year-old man with diminished lung capacity (decades earlier he lost part of one lung to surgery following an infection), sciatica, and an entire world demanding that he go here, do this, don't do that as well as expecting him to bring a little relief to our souls and peace to our world — and he had not yet had a mental breakdown.

I would have had a mental breakdown.

I was experiencing some of what I imagined he was experiencing, but on a vastly smaller scale, and I was a mess.

I felt like I had basically no working lungs (thanks to my never-ending battle with bronchitis).

My entire body hurt (thanks to my recent difficult pregnancy and birth experience).

And I had my own very vocal group of small followers who were demanding that I do this (shoelaces and cereal), don't do this (bedtime and naps), bring a little relief to their souls (thank you, Blue Bell ice cream) and peace to their world (stop hitting your sister, please). Endlessly, 365 days a year.

But where he was peaceful, I was anxious.

THE *WHO* AND THE *WHY*

There never seemed to be nearly enough time to accomplish everything on my to-do list when I was healthy and didn't have a newborn. How I was supposed to keep things running smoothly while dealing with an immune system that had gone AWOL and a baby who, though utterly delicious, was also utterly helpless, I wasn't entirely sure.

Pope Francis didn't seem too concerned with the "hows," though. He also didn't seem too hung up on the "whats," the "wheres," or the "whens." He seemed content to leave that to his handlers and, if necessary, let everyone practice the virtue of patience for a bit. Over and over again he demonstrated that the people standing directly in front of him were more important than the dials on his watch.

What he did seem concerned with was the *who* and the *why*.

The *who* were his flock. The homeless with whom he ate lunch. The schoolteacher who couldn't stop kissing him. The children who broke through the barriers, dodging left and right to avoid security, bound and determined to give a drawing to their papa. With each embrace his smile grew more radiant and the twinkle in his eye a little more mischievous. He had come for his people, and they had come for him; and for those brief moments when he was face to face with them, it seemed that all was right in his world.

As for the *why*, well it was simple, I suppose. Because God has asked him to feed his flock. And so, though the hours in the day were almost as numbered as the loaves and fishes, feed them he would. That I understood.

What continued to elude me was how — with everything he needed to accomplish and with all the pressure that he was under — he managed to remain so peaceful. Because I didn't carry even a fraction of the expectations on my shoulders that he did and peaceful wouldn't have been the first word that came to mind had I been asked to describe my current state of mind.

I had no doubt, of course, that Pope Francis, in the privacy of his room and personal thoughts, was battling his own demons. We all must and do. I was sure he experienced fear, anxiety, anger, and impatience like the rest of us. But he didn't let it paralyze him or dictate his actions. The same couldn't have been said of me.

I wanted to know his secrets.

I wiped up a puddle of milk that I had spilled while preparing dinner, reminded Charlie (who could always be counted on to tend to the duties of his two-year-old state in life with aplomb) that in our culture we sit in chairs, not on the top of the table, and settled down to watch the canonization.

As I sat there watching the coverage — feet propped up on a chair, messy hair in a bun, and troublingly dark circles under my eyes — I heard God whisper in that subtle way of his, "Pay attention, sweet Hallie. This is important."

I blocked out the cacophony that surrounded me just in time to hear Pope Francis wrap up his homily:

Father Serra had a motto which inspired his life and work, not just a saying, but above all a reality which shaped the way he lived: *siempre adelante!* Keep moving forward! For him, this was the way to continue experiencing the joy of the Gospel, to keep his heart from growing numb, from being anesthetized.

He kept moving forward, because the Lord was waiting. He kept going, because his brothers and sisters were waiting. He kept going forward to the end of his life. Today, like him, may we be able to say: Forward! Let's keep moving forward!

Junipero Serra was a man who, like Pope Francis, had been assigned a mighty job by God. Born in Spain, he hopped aboard a ship and sailed to Vera Cruz, Mexico, at the age of thirty-five. When he arrived, instead of riding the horses that had been provided for him and his fellow friars, he elected to walk the 250 miles to Mexico City. (Clearly a call from God because who would choose that kind of craziness?) Over the course of his life he would learn new languages, found and then assist in the building of at least ten new missions, travel to California to continue his evangelistic work, and suffer from no small number of injuries and ailments.

But he kept moving forward. *Siempre adelante!*

ONE FOOT IN FRONT OF THE OTHER

I immediately sensed that this was what God wanted me to meditate on. My vocation hadn't yet asked me to travel across countries on foot, but it seemed to me that it did require a commitment to constant forward motion. Ask any mother, and she will tell you that she doesn't stop moving much from dawn to dusk (and often right through again to dawn). There are mouths to feed, cheeks to kiss, eyes to dry, laundry to fold, errands to run, bills to be paid, appointments to book, diapers to be changed, and that's just the beginning.

During one particularly chaotic season, I made a home management binder in an effort to bring order to my days. It was covered in green and blue and featured cutouts of tiny birds. It read: "Bless This Nest." Among other things, it contained a day-by-day, detailed hourly schedule. Rise at six, pray, make a hot breakfast, clean the kitchen, take the children on a walk, mop the floors, and so on. That's all well and good (as were my intentions) if you are a person who can create such a plan without becoming a slave to it.

I could not.

That binder, which I had spent so much time creating, tortured me. If I missed a step, I felt like a failure. If I didn't miss a step but the children came behind and undid what I had spent so much time and energy doing, I felt like all of my efforts had been in vain. No matter how hard I tried, at the end of the day I was demoralized and angry. So I gave up entirely. Frustrated with my failure to complete my to-do list perfectly, and determined to stop venting that frustration onto my loved ones, I threw my to-do list into the trash and learned to ignore the chaos that was springing up all around me.

This had all the negative repercussions you might expect. So, like the good father he is, God had taken pity on me and was showing me another way.

"Hallie," he said, "I'm not expecting perfection from you, or even success. Just be faithful, and all will be well."

If there were not enough hours in my day to complete my list of tasks, if circumstances kept me from accomplishing whatever I felt needed to be accomplished, it was not a failure of mine, it was because I was trying to do something that was not the will of God. That was what he wanted me to understand.

It seems so blindingly obvious, and yet this truth escaped me for so long: God will never fail to give me the time I need to complete the jobs that he assigns to me. All of my fear and frustration had been born of a failure to trust that if I simply stayed close to God and put one foot in front of the other, he would sustain me and bless my efforts.

Pope Francis knew this when he came to America. He lived his life in the moment, always open to whatever assignment God laid at his feet, and he didn't let unexpected and less than ideal circumstances throw him. If God prompted him to comfort a widow, then clearly it was God's will that the meeting should wait. If he was tired and needed a nap, then something else would have to be struck from the calendar. And if people got upset about it, well then, they could take it up with God. He was going to keep moving forward.

There are different seasons in family life. Some are messy and some are clean, some lonely and some so far from lonely that they leave you wanting to pull your hair out. They all serve a purpose. They all have lessons woven into them. The key to my finding peace was to not let perfection become the enemy of the good and to trust in God's wise plans for my days and nights. To keep moving forward even if that meant nothing more than giving one more hug or wiping one more nose.

The season I found myself in when Pope Francis came to visit was a peanut-butter-and-jelly, antibiotics-heavy, messy one. My health and house were a disaster and my energy low. But I learned a great lesson during this time. I learned that completed to-do lists and sparkling, lemon-scented floors are wonderful when they appear (and they will, elusive though they may sometimes seem), but that the most important thing of all is that my home be a place of love. If my to-do list is inhibiting this, it's time to take a deep breath and ask God to reveal his will and reorient me. For in the end, it is love that will propel us toward heaven, and that is, after all, the most important forward motion of all.

Siempre adelante!

❧ CHAPTER NINE

Slow Work

**Have patience to walk with short steps
until you have wings to fly.**

~ St. Francis de Sales

I loved late winter when I was a girl. Every day I would race barefoot down our gravel driveway, past the grapevines, and below the heavy-hanging boughs of our evergreen to find our mailbox full to bursting with colorful gardening catalogs. On some days our postman — a friendly old man who never failed to greet me with a smile — would bring us catalogs covered in colorful blossoms, and on other days, fruit and vegetable or supply catalogs.

I can still remember so vividly my mother sitting in bed with her comforter pulled up to her chin, a catalog in her lap, and yellow sticky notes scattered about her as she pored over each page. You could almost see the ideas blossoming in her mind as with furrowed brow and bitten lip, she planned her garden on loose-leaf. She had half of an acre to work with and still, I suspect, could not find room for everything she wanted to grow. Pumpkins, green beans, strawberries, zucchini, and endless varieties of flowers — all of which needed a home — jockeyed for space.

The only things she never omitted were the two miniature roses that sat in planters next to our porch swing, one for me and one for my younger sister. Each year a new variety, but always a rose with a name, color, or other quality that reminded her of us. All winter I looked forward to the day that she would bring my new rose home and reveal why she had made the choice she had. I couldn't wait, in that singular way that young girls can't wait for anything, to find out what it was about this tiny, velvety, sweet-smelling rose that made her think of me.

Together we would drag out a wooden barrel and a bag of soil, and she would show me how to give my little rose a new home, reminding me that I needed to water it daily and keep a careful watch for aphids. If I was patient, and took good care of it, she said, my little spindly branched plant would bloom into a beautiful bush of roses.

To this day it remains a mystery to me why that little girl — who had such great faith in herself and her ability to guide those rose bushes to life with her imperfect hands — grew into a woman who had such little faith in herself and in God who was (and is) guiding her to life with his perfect hands.

For a long time, though, that was me. Fearing that, love God though I did, I might be a hopeless case destined to be stuck in the muck and mire of human fallenness forever. Fearing that I would never learn to love God more perfectly, and my fellow man even decently. Fearing that I would never stop stumbling and falling. And fearing that one day God would give up on me entirely and walk away, frustrated with my pathetic — and often apathetic — efforts at sanctity.

I never yelled at my little roses, castigating them for growing too slowly. Part of the joy was the waiting — for a new bud to emerge from between leaves or for a hint of color from inside the bud, but I yelled at myself all the time for failing to make swift enough progress in the spiritual life.

I never felt despondent upon discovering that a swarm of aphids had launched an attack or a fungus had taken a liking to my roses' leaves. Rather, I would find it a challenge. It would invigorate me, coaxing me to fight harder on behalf of my little roses. The same couldn't have been said of my response to spiritual challenges. More often than not, rather than stand my ground and fight, I would grow depressed, draw the blinds, and take to bed, chick lit, chocolate, and a box of tissues in hand.

And I never doubted that one morning in late summer I would step out onto my porch to find my little plant covered with luscious blossoms. Not once.

But for a long time I doubted every day that I would become the woman of God that I yearned to be. I couldn't see that just as my roses had to wait season after season to reach their full potential, so would I.

GOD IS NOT IN A HURRY

I think God knows that there are things his beloved creatures can't do without on their long spiritual journeys. Things like winter, which forces us into our homes to curl up by the fire and spend some time in quiet contemplation. Spring, which bursts forth with signs of new life to give us hope when we're feeling defeated. Hot, arid summers, which prompt us to seek sustenance in spiritual food and water. And fall, the season of harvest, in which we are given the opportunity to share the fruit of our labors with others. These are all good things. Things that cannot be rushed.

God is not in a hurry, it would seem. But I am.

Every time I go to Confession I leave feeling like all of my brokenness — the gaping cracks and ragged edges —

have been filled up and smoothed over with grace. There has never been a time when I have stepped out of the confessional not feeling like a miracle has just occurred. But I don't remember the details of each experience. Some stick, though, making their way into my mind over and over again. No doubt this is God's work, reminding me of lessons learned that I need to meditate on over and over again.

I have never forgotten the affectionate laugh of a particularly wise priest when I unburdened my heart to him and shared my frustration at making so little spiritual progress. I told him that I'd been working so hard to be more disciplined and had even created a daily prayer schedule.

"Tell me about this schedule," he said.

"Well," I replied, "my plan was to rise with the sun for private prayer, pray with the children before breakfast, pray again briefly midmorning and midafternoon, as a family after dinner, and privately again before bed. Prayer before meals, as well, of course. That was my plan. But I have yet to be successful at it even once. Not even once, Father, and it's not for lack of trying!"

That's when the affectionate laugh came into play.

"And you've been Catholic for how long?"

"About seven years."

"I see. Well, you're young, and I know that seven years probably feels like a long time, but you're really still a baby Catholic. There's nothing wrong with any of the things you've planned — they are all beautiful, important spiritual practices — but I think you may be trying to take on too much. Think of it this way: if you hadn't exercised for many years and decided that you wanted to run a marathon, you wouldn't lace up your shoes and expect to be able to run twenty-six miles. That would be crazy, but that's essentially what you're trying to do with this schedule. If you wanted to run a marathon you'd probably start out by running a few blocks and then work up to a mile and then add another mile and so on. Try taking a similar approach with your schedule. Start with blessings at meal times and maybe a brief morning consecration and an evening examination of conscience. Once you've made these things a habit, add in a Rosary or one of the Liturgies of the Hours. But go slow. Be patient with yourself."

The problem with going to Saturday afternoon Confession with everyone else is that you don't have a lot of time to argue with your confessor. If I'd had more time, I could have told him that God had shown me a great mercy when he led me to Christianity and that I had quite a lot to prove to him. I could have told him that God had given me more of an all-or-nothing personality and that "all" was the only option, unless we wanted to go with "nothing," but I figured that we agreed that wasn't the ideal choice. I could have told him all sorts of things that might have given him pause, but God in all his wisdom decided that this Confession should leave just enough time for me to listen. Later, I could reflect.

The priest's advice stuck, and it was still percolating — and I was still arguing — when, years later, I read an interview with an iconographer. This iconographer spoke of creating an icon as a journey and was emphatic that the process of creating was almost as important as the end product. He said that he was often tempted to race to the finish line but that he was learning to trust in the slow work of God. His art had taught him, he said, that we can't rush the business of living or creating, for each individual step and stroke contains a lesson worth savoring.

I might have been tempted to argue with him, too, but the words "the slow work of God" stopped me in my tracks. Suddenly I understood that I'd been looking at the process of spiritual growth entirely wrong. I'd been approaching it as if everything relied on my ability to summon ever-increasing amounts of self-discipline, zeal, and fortitude. But I came to understand that to approach spiritual growth in such a way fails to take into account that on this earthly journey we constantly travel from valley to mountaintop, through ever-changing seasons.

I've had moments atop mountains when, yes, I was able to summon all the fortitude and fervor my heart desired. But I've also spent a lot of time in the valley. And in the valleys, I struggle. When loved ones are sick, babies resist sleep, bank accounts are empty, or the weight of the world feels heavy on my shoulders, my prayers are simple, desperate pleas.

"Please, God, lead this baby to the Land of Nod."

"Heal her."

"Help him."

"I cannot do this anymore."

"I'm so incredibly angry with you. Why won't you fix this?"

And sometimes, when words fail me entirely, "Lord, have mercy. Christ, have mercy. Lord, have mercy." Over and over again.

ON THE WAY TO THE UNKNOWN

What I've slowly come to understand is that these cold, dark seasons are not useless. They don't point to a failure on my part to be holy. If anything, they make me more honest. They strip me of platitudes and false humility and bring me to my knees before God, pummeling the dirt with my fists and settling the dust with my tears. They strip me of pride and, left completely spent and with nowhere else to turn, lift my lined face toward my Maker.

These seasons are not prayer-schedule friendly. But they are every bit as essential to spiritual growth as the seasons that allow me to meditate deeply for long periods of time. These are the seasons that teach me to let go and surrender. And if the years since my conversion have taught me anything, it is that spiritual growth is synonymous with spiritual surrender.

We grow spiritually as our trust in God grows. We grow as, little by little, we loosen our grip and align our will with his. And we grow as we recognize that from him comes all goodness — the sparkle in our children's eyes, the warm sun on our skin, ripe peaches, the high of new love and the comfort of mature love, bread and wine turned to Body and Blood, everything.

We grow as we surrender to the *slow* work of God.

As a mother of seven, I am the last person who would bemoan modern conveniences. I love that on hard nights I can have a pizza delivered in mere minutes, hugely grateful that I can hop on a plane and, within hours, be wrapping far-away friends and family members in a hug, and I would be lost without my washer and dryer that takes our massive pile (truly, you have no idea) of dirty laundry and makes it sweet smelling in no time at all. I count all of these things among my choicest blessings, but there is no doubt that such advantages have made us an impatient people.

Impatient not only with the frustrations of daily life, but also with our own slow forward movement in the spiritual life. We want to have been counted among the saints yesterday. We want to flip a switch and have our souls light up, instantaneously free of sin and full of grace.

Or at least I do.

God's preference has always been to give me little bits of wisdom, one at time. He lets me play with them a bit, then gathers them up, pieces them together, and hands the completed project to me in one glorious ah-ha moment.

This time it came by way of Pierre Teilhard de Chardin, S.J., who I believe, for all his questionable ideas, was one with the Spirit when he wrote this poem:

> Above all, trust in the slow work of God.
> We are quite naturally impatient in everything
> to reach the end without delay.
> We should like to skip the intermediate stages.
> We are impatient of being on the way to something
> unknown, something new.
> And yet it is the law of all progress
> that it is made by passing through
> some stages of instability —
> and that it may take a very long time.
>
> And so I think it is with you;
> your ideas mature gradually — let them grow,
> let them shape themselves, without undue haste.
> Don't try to force them on,
> as though you could be today what time
> (that is to say, grace and circumstances
> acting on your own good will)
> will make of you tomorrow.
>
> Only God could say what this new spirit
> gradually forming within you will be.
> Give Our Lord the benefit of believing
> that his hand is leading you,
> and accept the anxiety of feeling yourself
> in suspense and incomplete.

If I had been tempted to dismiss the advice of the priest who told me to be patient with myself, or the wise words of the iconographer to trust in the slow work of God, the discovery of this poem left me with no room to argue. It seemed to me the perfect consolidation of all the wisdom that the Holy Spirit had been feeding me over the years and a flawless formula for finding peace when the devil on my shoulder whispers that my progress is pathetically insufficient and my heart hopelessly cold.

My heart is cold, it is true, but God is not going to leave it that way. He holds it in his hands and warms it, and each day a new small corner thaws and springs to life. I may not be able to feel it on a day-to-day basis, but that's where faith comes in.

Recently, on a rock-bottom sort of day, I cried out to God with tears in my eyes and said, "You are sucking the life out of me!" Ever so gently he replied, "No, my girl. I'm sucking the death out of you. And into you, I'm pouring my love."

God meant it when he promised not to abandon us or leave us orphans. He will be with us in the dark valleys and on the euphoric peaks. He will sustain us during icy cold winters and give us drink during stifling hot summers. He will satisfy our every hunger, and he will pour new life into our spirits. And just as I did for my tiny roses, he will give us everything we need to bloom.

All that he asks is that we take his hand.

CHAPTER TEN

Compass

Safe?… Who said anything about safe? 'Course he isn't safe. But he's good. He's the King, I tell you.

~ C. S. Lewis

Several years ago my sweet Louisiana-born-and-bred grandmother casually mentioned — as if simply retelling a story she once heard — that she'd almost been in a plane crash once. She and my grandfather had been passengers in my great-uncle's small plane and were soaring over Texas when the engines suddenly went out. Dead silence filled the cabin, and the plane began to descend.

Horrified — not being a huge fan of air travel to begin with — I asked her if she had been scared. How had she managed to keep her heart from stopping out of sheer terror? Did a Janet Leigh-esque scream escape her lips and threaten to shatter the windows? Was she overwhelmed by grief?

She thought for a moment, laughed, and said that no, strangely enough she had not been scared at all. In fact, she had felt completely at peace. She had lived a good life, she said, and she was ready to go if it was God's will.

Obviously, since she lived to tell the tale, the engines somehow sprang back to life. She even climbed aboard other planes and continued to fly the friendly skies for many years afterward. (I'm still processing this information.)

More recently, my beautiful red-headed friend Jen found herself gasping for breath and was rushed to the hospital. She was pregnant at the time and was concerned that, given her blood-clotting disorder, clots might have formed in her legs and traveled up to her lungs. She knew that this could be fatal. In fact, her doctor had told her that if a clot were to lodge itself in her lungs, she would have a mere hour, if she was lucky, to get help.

Upon arriving, they hooked her up to an IV line, ran dye through her veins, and gave her a CT scan. Generally, the results of such a test can only be read by a specialist, but two of the many clots in her lungs were so large that the physician on duty was able to immediately spot them. Jen was admitted to the hospital on the spot.

While there, she met an orderly who told her that a few weeks prior, he had taken care of a man who, like her, had been diagnosed with bilateral pulmonary embolisms. He didn't have nearly as many clots as she did, though, the man said. Knowing well how serious pulmonary embolisms are, and looking for a little reassurance, Jen asked how he was doing now. The orderly paused and said, "Oh, well, he died."

My jaw dropped open as Jen relayed this story, and I inundated her with questions similar to the ones I'd bombarded my grandmother with. Was she terrified? Did she collapse from the shock of it all? And how had she managed to refrain from throwing the nearest hard object at the orderly's head?

She laughed, just as my grandmother had, and said that she had actually felt surprisingly calm at the time. She loved God and knew that he loved her, and she trusted in his will even if it meant that it was her time to go. She, too, had been at peace in the midst of what sounded to me to be an unfathomably terrible experience.

TURN YOUR IMAGINATION
TOWARD THE LIGHT

I used to spend a lot of time, no doubt much more than I should have, imagining how I would react should a variety of worst-case scenarios play out in my life. I imagined histrionics. I imagined utter despair. And I imagined richly colored velvet fainting couches and smelling salts. What I didn't often imagine was peace.

It's a wonderful gift, the ability to wonder and imagine. But as with so many gifts I've been given, I wasn't nearly as careful with it as I should have been, and for a time it caused me no small amount of anxiety.

I have always been a bit of a hypochondriac. Lingering coughs are probably lung cancer, and the occasional feeling of pins and needles in my hand, likely a sign of permanent nerve damage. Or worse. (Google is always happy to help with my efforts at self-diagnosis.) I am also, as I mentioned, afraid of being in a plane crash, being murdered in my bed, and of having a loved one die prematurely. When I was young, I went through a phase in which I read a seemingly endless series of novels about teenagers who had cancer, and I spent several years sleeping on my mother's bedroom floor after hearing on the news that a local girl had been kidnapped. My fears had hijacked my imagination — and by extension my life — and drove it in a very dark direction.

When God created each of us, he tucked a little bit of his divine imagination into our souls. He did this, I think, so that we can conceive of the fact that our world contains so much more than we can see, feel, and touch. But my imagination didn't take these things of beauty and reveal to me the holiness hidden in creation. No, my imagination was like a filmstrip full of macabre, terrifying possibilities.

Death without grace, danger without consolation, and sickness with no hope of temporal or heavenly relief.

Once upon a time, the Hebrew people handed down stories of God orally, as their friends and family sat round breathing in the details and bringing them to life in their minds. Then came Christ, indisputably the greatest lover of stories, weaving parables before the eyes and ears of his followers, desperate to give them an even deeper understanding of divine realities. And now we have the Church, who is still telling us God's stories but also feeding us with his Flesh and Blood, cleansing us of our sins with holy water, and exciting our senses with stained glass, rosary beads, incense, votive candles, religious medals, and divinely inspired art. All of these things fortify us and keep our attention focused where it needs to be as we stumble our way toward salvation.

God knew that we would need vivid imaginations to take these gifts — the stories, sacraments, and sacramentals — and allow them to reach their full potential in our lives. He knew, dare I say, that we would need imagination to see *reality*; and he intends, I think, for us to use it as a sort of compass, guiding us along our path to heaven. Mine had cracked a bit, because I hadn't guarded it sufficiently, and darkness had seeped in. But God makes all things new, so he sealed the cracks and polished it up a bit and taught me how to use it well. (First lesson: break up with Google.)

I thought a lot about the moment Peter walked on water as I was recalibrating my compass. There he is doing something absolutely crazy, a terribly ill-conceived plan if there ever was one; but his eyes are on Jesus, and things are going pretty well. But then he gets distracted by the storm — which is understandable since this wasn't just any storm but a *seismos*, to use Matthew's choice of a Greek word, a "shaking, a tempest, and an earthquake." He looks away for a moment, overcome by fear, and he starts to sink into the lake. He cries out for help, afraid of drowning, and there, in the blink of an eye, is Jesus stretching out his hand to save him and saying, "O you of little faith, why did you doubt?" (Mt 14:31).

People like to tease the apostles for being such a bumbling, easily confused lot, but let me tell you, I probably wouldn't have asked Jesus to let me walk on water to begin with. He was already headed in the direction of the boat. I could have waited, I think, for him to make his way over, and then we could have settled the ghost versus God issue.

But Peter asked, and he walked, and as long as his focus was on God, he was fine. It was as I heard this Gospel passage read at Mass that I realized my imagination had gone astray when it had begun to show me a world devoid of God's presence.

IT TAKES A VILLAGE

My friend Jen survived her bilateral pulmonary embolisms, thank God, but her trials during that pregnancy were far from over. In the early morning on a mid-April day her labor began. Jen and I stay in close contact, and I knew that when I hadn't heard from her by early afternoon that something had gone wrong. I was right. The labor was extremely difficult and involved thirteen blood draws in one arm, a startlingly incompetent nurse, and ended with her newborn son being ripped from her arms and taken to the ICU when he developed breathing problems.

The pediatricians on staff determined that her son had holes in both his lungs and would need to be transferred to a higher-level hospital. Before he was whisked away, Jen caught sight of him in an incubator, wrapped in dozens of wires, red faced and screaming, desperate to be held by his mother. She was not allowed to touch him, and as they wheeled him away, Jen thought she might never see her son alive again.

She sat empty-armed on her hospital bed, utterly spent, having just offered up everything she had inside of her to bring her son into the world after a brutally traumatizing pregnancy. She had barely even had a chance to hold him, to whisper into his fuzzy ears how much his mama loved him, or to sniff his newborn neck with the scent of heaven still fresh in the folds, and now there was a distinct possibility that she never would. She maintains that it was the darkest moment of her life.

Unlike when she had first been diagnosed with bilateral pulmonary embolisms, she felt none of God's grace. The only thing that kept her company in that cold room was unspeakable anger and immeasurable grief.

God understood. He wasn't angry with her for being angry with him. He didn't turn his back on her and walk away. Instead, he sat quietly in the corner of her hospital room and called a small army into action.

The first to arrive was a nurse who happened to be a fellow parishioner of Jen's. This nurse made sure that she was not woken up every fifteen minutes, allowing Jen to get some desperately needed sleep (something that had never happened during any of her previous hospital stays). When it was time for a shift change, God sent in a new nurse who was the mother of a priest and had not only been at a retreat that Jen had attended, but had actually been part of her four-member small group at the event. This woman was not supposed to be at the hospital that day but due to some totally unexpected mishap was called into work. In myriad ways, she went above and beyond, pushing the limits of hospital protocol, to make sure that Jen had everything she needed.

Next in the unexpected turn of events, Jen's primary doctor was unable to come into the hospital that day, so he sent his wife, also a physician, to check on her. This woman, too, was a faithful Catholic. Shortly thereafter, God sent Jen's friend Kathryn, who, having once had a baby in the NICU herself, knew that even though Jen hadn't asked for visitors, she should come. As it turned out, if Kathryn had not arrived, Jen would not have been able to go visit her son. And then, just to make sure that Jen saw God's hand in all of this and felt his unwavering love for her, Jen's priest arrived.

So, before Jen knew what had hit her, she found herself surrounded by the body of Christ who comforted her and said for her the prayers that she could not at that moment utter.

After she and her son had both made a full recovery, I asked her whether this experience had been as bad as she might have imagined it to be. She said that it was actually worse than she would have envisioned and reemphasized that it felt like God was nowhere to be found. But then she paused and said that there were elements involved — signal graces that pointed to God's presence even though she herself could not feel him near at that moment — that were unexpected. Good things, like the people who had come to her hospital room and lifted her up in companionship and prayer. When she imagined her worst nightmares playing out, she wouldn't have thought to include those.

STEPPING INTO REALITY

Jen's story showed me that while in some challenging moments God will feel so close that you can almost sense his arms wrapped around you, not every hardship is going to be accompanied by a tangible awareness of his presence.

Perhaps he knew that what Jen needed most after her son was born was to see that she had a village surrounding and supporting her, so he humbly stepped aside and let his people care for her.

Or maybe he had a different reason entirely. Maybe there were other lessons wrapped up in that experience that are for Jen, and Jen alone, to unpack, wrestle with, and eventually savor. What I know is this: God is endlessly creative, has perfect knowledge of what we need in order to grow closer to him, and will make sure that we get those things.

That we will suffer in this life is a certainty. People lose children, are tortured, and watch everything they hold dear go up in smoke all over the world every day. It would be cruel to discount their suffering with empty platitudes about God's comforting grace. Suffering is real, and it is often brutal. But it would also do an injustice to God's goodness to deny that he is always with us in some mystical way even though we may not always be able to feel him near.

I used to wonder where God was in those moments when I felt paralyzed by fear. Where was the deliverance from my anxiety I yearned for? Why did I feel so terribly alone? What I finally came to understand is that God gives grace for the situation, not the imagination. These fears I had weren't based in reality. They were like dark fairy tales that had escaped from inside well-worn covers and had somehow tricked me into believing that their stories were real. To find God's grace, I needed to step back into reality.

We cannot always control what happens to us in this life. Our time on this earth promises to be both more beautiful and more tragic than we could ever imagine. What we can control is whether we let fear steal our moments of peace, joy, and happiness. That is for us to choose.

May we guard our compasses well.

CHAPTER ELEVEN

With Gratitude

I can, with one eye squinted, take it all as a blessing.
~ Flannery O'Connor

I sometimes tell people that Dan and I live paycheck to paycheck, but that really doesn't quite describe our financial situation. It is more like: paycheck to utter pennilessness, which lasts at least twenty-four to seventy-two hours, followed by another paycheck, and repeat. Over the course of our married life, we have had utilities turned off, been threatened with eviction, spent more time without health insurance than with, dug crumb-covered coins out of car cup holders and couch cushions to buy groceries, begged for money from loved ones, and accrued more debt than I care to think about.

I have a hard time describing us as poor because, after all, we live in the United States — being poor in the land of plenty isn't the same as being poor in other parts of the world. Still, I could safely put it this way: if poverty was a beloved lady to St. Francis, she is, to us, an annoying next-door neighbor who is always stopping by unexpectedly to say hello.

For a long time this made me feel very scared. I think everyone has a moment in their lives when their illusion of control is demolished and they come face-to-face with the reality that they are ultimately powerless. Usually this is the same moment in which they realize that everything, absolutely everything, relies upon God's goodness. If you can be counted among the slightly less trusting inhabitants of this world, as I can, this epiphany might even prompt you to turn to God and say, "I really hope you know what you're doing here."

Cancer diagnoses teach this lesson in short order. As do wars. And, as I discovered, poverty.

Not knowing where the money to keep the lights on or the pantry stocked will come from has a singular way of twisting one's insides into knots and demanding a level of bravery that I, as a young woman in my twenties, was not prepared to summon. I didn't want to find God hiding in the muck and mire of my life, I really just wanted him to lead us both out of it and into a life that included quite a few more overpriced Starbuck's beverages. It didn't seem to me, at the time, to be too much to ask.

During one of the many financially lean times that Dan and I endured over the years, we had to give up our Internet connection for a while. This, tragically, was before either of us owned a smartphone, so we couldn't even get our Internet fix via our phones (not that we would have been able to pay to keep those on, either, of course).

Email was received and sent, and social media checked, at a McDonald's up the road that had free Wi-Fi. I've always loved the Internet, but back then, when I was in the thick of young motherhood, it was a lifeline to the outside world that I relied on to keep me sane. There are many dark corners lurking around the World Wide Web, but there are also sunny little café-esque spots where the lonely can convene and share little bits and pieces of their lives over a virtual cup of coffee. Those were the spots I frequented, and I missed them immensely.

I was talking to a friend on the phone during this time, and I said, "You know, the worst part of it all is that I'm not even making the most of this Internet fast. I'm not reading great books, or taking my kids on adventure walks, or spending more time in prayer. I haven't stumbled upon or searched for any deep spiritual insights. I basically just wipe bottoms, fill bottles, and then stare at the wall."

In the days after those words left my mouth, it hit me that this was kind of a problem. God had led us to a life of humble means when we discerned that he was calling Dan to work for the Church. We've never regretted that decision, nor second-guessed it. Dan was (and is) good at what he does. He meets people where they are, with true care in his heart, and leads them to Christ. He's the guy who runs into a homeless man on the street and not only buys him lunch, but eats with him and then gives him the coat off his back and tries to find him housing. He's the one who stays until midnight with his students after teaching a class to continue answering questions and offering support, even though he has to be up at dawn. He is exactly where he is meant to be. But where he is not is in a particularly lucrative spot. Certainly not one that comes with (earthly) profit sharing.

I needed to accept that if God had called us to this life — and he did — then he had also called us to all of the circumstances that came with it, knowing in that all-knowing way of his, that this was the perfect place to plant us. This was where we would thrive. All the little crosses we were carrying had been fashioned, down to their very last splinter, with us in mind.

In other words, I needed to stop staring at the wall.

SUNLIGHT SLICING THROUGH HAZE

I heard someone say once that our mind can only process fifty bits of information at a time. As it turns out, this is false. The claim apparently stemmed from an obscure study made many decades ago that was taken out of context. The experts now say the processing ability of the mind cannot be measured in bits per second. But it got me thinking. I think there is some truth to the idea that our minds have a limited capacity for processing information at any given moment. And at this moment in time, my mind was processing an awful lot of fearful thoughts.

This made me wonder if I couldn't force some of those thoughts out of my mind by replacing them with something else. Something better. If, when my trust wavered and my courage balked, I chose to instead think about good and happy things, maybe there wouldn't be so much space left in my head for the scary things. So I started talking to God about this theory of mine. I told him that since I couldn't distract myself from my anxieties with good things like island vacations and shopping trips to Target, perhaps he could give me some other suggestions.

He laughed, as if he had been waiting an extraordinarily long time for me to ask, and said, "Gratitude, my girl. Fight fear with gratitude."

When I was worried about how we were going to pay for our next bag of groceries or buy Christmas presents for the kids, when I dug down deep for courage and came up empty-handed, when I tried to place all my trust in him and failed, he said to find something to be grateful for and offer thanks.

And so I did. Just for little things at first. Thank you for the rain. Thank you for our little downtown library and the mom-and-pop shops that we pass on our way there. Thank you for my daughter's round rosy cheeks and the flowers my boys pick and present so proudly to me. Thank you for sea-salt-covered dark chocolate and for strawberries. Thank you for children who take long naps. Oh, and thank you for novels that let me get lost in their pages. Those are the best.

Thomas Merton once said that gratitude "is constantly awakening to a new wonder." This was my experience as well. As soon as I started looking around for things for which to be grateful, they seemed to be everywhere. It was as if fear had been a fog that had shrouded my eyes, and gratitude, like rays of the sun, was slicing through the haze. I suddenly saw everything in a new light. Even the things I once feared, like our perpetually empty bank account, revealed blessings when I looked at them through the eyes of gratitude.

Fear told me that no one else had as many struggles as we did because they were all having their prayers answered the instant they hit their knees. Why? Well, because God loved them more than me, of course.

But gratitude opened my eyes to the fact that we are all perpetually cycling through seasons of plenty and seasons of want. When I am planting seeds in dry earth, my friend may be harvesting basket after basket of rich fruit. And when she is sitting in a torrential downpour, I may be savoring the warm sun. All of these things — the heat and cold, aridity and fertility, times of want and plenty — are essential to our spiritual growth, but God, in all of his unfathomable wisdom, probably sat down one day and tried to imagine all of us down on earth living lives of perfect synchronicity. The happy seasons would be lovely, euphoric even, but can you imagine what would happen if we all had to walk through the dark valleys of life simultaneously?

Well, at any rate, God could, and he realized what a very poor plan that would be. He knew that when I feel dry as a bone, I need my fruit-bearing sister to pull me to my feet and share her bounty. And when she stumbles and falls, blinded by whatever merciless storm she's walking through, she needs me to hold her up and guide her with Christ's light.

Fear also stole my perspective. It held up all of my crosses before me and asked me if I realized how unbearably hard my life was. Did I know that my crosses were heavier, and my life harder, than the crosses and lives of everyone else?

Gratitude laughed in the face of fear and showed me how unspeakably blessed I was with my small enchanting children dancing by my side and my beloved husband in my bed. It gently guided my focus away from my own small crosses and revealed the truly agonizing hardships present in the lives of others. It coaxed me to open my heart and taught me to pray for the sick, starving, and suffering of the world.

Fear told me that I should be ashamed of my old car, my small house, my worn-out dresses, and my reliance on others.

Gratitude showed me the beauty of interdependence. As I began to share my struggles with others, they felt free to share theirs with me. Before I knew it, we were passing hand-me-downs back and forth, raiding our pantries and uniting the random ingredients to make a meal, and quietly tucking money into one another's purses whenever we were able.

Fear pointed to all of the things I didn't have.

Gratitude made me appreciate the things I did. I learned to savor the taste of a cold tangerine, freshly picked from my yard, and treasure the vintage dress found hiding behind all the other dresses at the thrift store. No longer did I take things for granted. My appreciation for all of God's little gifts swelled and soared, and I found myself enjoying them so much more than I had when everything I desired was available to me with the swipe of a card.

Fear stole my memory and made me forget how much God had done for me.

Gratitude reminded me that God had yet to abandon me in my hour of need. It reminded me that like any good father, God wanted me to come to him with all my struggles. When we didn't have money for a car repair, or food, or new clothes, I prayed. When I had a problem that only the money that we didn't have could fix, I prayed. When all possible solutions to a problem had been tried and had failed, I prayed. And when children were sick, my husband was tired, my friends heartbroken, I prayed.

THE FULLNESS OF LIFE

During World War II, a woman named Corrie ten Boom and her family opened their home to refugees, hiding them on the second floor in a secret room. Her father, Casper, had decreed that in his household, "God's people are always welcome," and so, though they knew well the consequences, they persisted.

In February 1944, they were arrested. Corrie and her sister, Betsie, were sent to the Ravensbrück concentration camp.

Corrie's memoir, *The Hiding Place*, chronicles their experience. As I read excerpts of her book, I was gobsmacked by how steadfast and strong their faith remained even while they were imprisoned, with their stomachs distended by hunger and the heaviness of death surrounding them. They faced each new horror not by doubting God's existence or goodness, as I suspect I would have, but instead by begging God for guidance. No issue was too small to bring to God's attention. Not even fleas. She wrote:

> "Fleas!" I cried. "Betsie, the place is swarming with them!"
>
> We scrambled across the intervening platforms, heads low to avoid another bump, dropped down to the aisle and hedged our way to a patch of light.
>
> "Here! And here another one!" I wailed. "Betsie, how can we live in such a place!"
>
> "Show us. Show us how." It was said so matter of factly it took me a second to realize she was praying. More and more the distinction between prayer and the rest of life seemed to be vanishing for Betsie.
>
> "Corrie!" she said excitedly. "He's given us the answer! Before we asked, as He always does! In the Bible this morning. Where was it? Read that part again!"
>
> I glanced down the long dim aisle to make sure no guard was in sight, then drew the Bible from its pouch. "It was in First Thessalonians," I said. We were on our third complete reading of the New Testament since leaving Scheveningen.
>
> In the feeble light I turned the pages. "Here it is: 'Comfort the frightened, help the weak, be patient with everyone. See that none of you repays evil for evil, but always seek to do

good to one another and to all....'" It seemed written expressly to Ravensbruck.

"Go on," said Betsie. "That wasn't all."

"Oh yes: ... 'Rejoice always, pray constantly, give thanks in all circumstances; for this is the will of God in Christ Jesus.'"

"That's it, Corrie! That's His answer. 'Give thanks in all circumstances!' That's what we can do. We can start right now to thank God for every single thing about this new barracks!" I stared at her; then around me at the dark, foul-aired room.

"Such as?" I said.

"Such as being assigned here together."

I bit my lip. "Oh yes, Lord Jesus!"

"Such as what you're holding in your hands." I looked down at the Bible.

"Yes! Thank You, dear Lord, that there was no inspection when we entered here! Thank You for all these women, here in this room, who will meet You in these pages."

"Yes," said Betsie, "Thank You for the very crowding here. Since we're packed so close, that many more will hear!" She looked at me expectantly. "Corrie!" she prodded.

"Oh, all right. Thank You for the jammed, crammed, stuffed, packed suffocating crowds."

"Thank You," Betsie went on serenely, "for the fleas and for —"

The fleas! This was too much. "Betsie, there's no way even God can make me grateful for a flea."

"Give thanks in all circumstances," she quoted. It doesn't say, "in pleasant circumstances." Fleas are part of this place where God has put us.

And so we stood between tiers of bunks and gave thanks for fleas. But this time I was sure Betsie was wrong."

The situation in the barracks only got worse as 1,400 women were stuffed into a building designed to hold 400. Corrie writes that there was constant fighting as the stench of overflowing toilets grew unbearable, lice spread from head to head, and fleas continued to torment. Desperate for relief, a few of the women began to pray for peace and almost immediately, a noticeable calm settled over the barracks. Their prayers grew more frequent and bold, but strangely the wardens never caught them worshipping.

One day Corrie came back from her work shift to find Betsie looking decidedly pleased with herself.

"You know, we've never understood why we had so much freedom in the big room," she said. "Well — I've found out."

That afternoon, she said, there'd been confusion in her knitting group about sock sizes and they'd asked the supervisor to come and settle it.

But she wouldn't. She wouldn't step through the door and neither would the guards. And you know why?

Betsie could not keep the triumph from her voice: "Because of the fleas! That's what she said, 'That place is crawling with fleas!'"

My mind rushed back to our first hour in this place. I remembered Betsie's bowed head, remembered her thanks to God for creatures I could see no use for."

As I read Corrie's story, I realized that when God told me to fight fear with gratitude, he didn't mean that I should be grateful for only the good and beautiful things in my life, he meant that I should be grateful for everything — for the suffering, the pain, the contempt, and the fear. Yes, even for the fear.

Fear isn't a bad thing in and of itself. Rational fear, for example, is one of our greatest allies as it serves to keep us safe and protect us from harm. If someone breaks into my house, it would probably be best if I didn't smile sweetly at him and invite him to tea. But even irrational fear, I was finding, had a purpose as long as I didn't allow it to rule or paralyze me. Which is what I had been doing as I stared at my walls. The words of a Mary Oliver poem echoed in my head: "Tell me, what is it you plan to do with your one wild and precious life?"

I wasn't sure exactly, but I knew that I didn't want to waste another day frozen by fear. So, I did what God had told me to do and started to list all of the things about fear for which I was grateful.

I was grateful that my fears had taught me how to have a little more compassion for others; grateful that they forced me to examine the dark, scary parts of my soul and bring them out into the light; grateful that they taught me about fortitude and endurance; and grateful that they showed me how to be completely dependent on God.

The truth is, life is brutal. This applies to the rich and poor, the healthy and not, and the happy and sad. No one gets a pass. We are all constantly being refined by fire and smoothed over by grace. But we do have a choice: we can embrace the fullness of life — birth and death, summer and winter, want and plenty, joy and grief — or we can turn in on ourselves, shutting out the world, letting fear paralyze us, and ultimately numbing ourselves so as not to feel anything at all.

Fear chooses the latter. But little by little, and day by day, I am learning to choose the former. With gratitude.

 CHAPTER TWELVE

Maximilian

**We have to be braver than we think we can be, because
God is constantly calling us to be more than we are.**
~ Madeleine L'Engle

God does funny things sometimes. Things like telling you
to host a conference, sitting quietly by while you select and
set the date for that conference, and then, as soon as you
do, sending a precious, tiny baby sailing down from heaven
who just happens to be due on the first day of that conference he told you to host.

Like I said, *funny*.

The good news was that this year's Edel Gathering
was taking place fifteen minutes away from my home in
a lovely old 1920s-era downtown Charleston hotel. Typi-
cally, I prefer to lock my front door, shutter the windows,
and barricade myself in my house starting at somewhere
around thirty-seven weeks of gestation. When you have a
cavalcade of brilliant, beautiful, spirited women coming to
town, though, that's not really an option. So instead I spent
the second half of my pregnancy hustling here, there, and
everywhere and made plans to spend my due date camped
out in a hotel.

Everyone asked me during the months leading up to
the event if I was scared. What if my water broke while I was

on the stage in front of a million women? (No. Just no.) Or worse yet, they said, what if I went into labor and, having a history of precipitous births, had that baby right there in the hotel? (Not worse, but okay.)

"I don't know," I replied, "would that be so bad?" A friend had taken an informal poll and determined that we'd have at least twenty doulas and probably a midwife or two in attendance. Perhaps we could even coax the debonair old man who played the hotel's grand piano on the weekends to serenade my little man with a rousing rendition of "Happy Birthday." No, if this baby chose to make an appearance, he would have a welcoming committee to end all welcoming committees. I wasn't worried about that.

What I was worried about was having my reputation ruined, being sued, draining my family's already small bank account, and/or leaving a large group of wonderful women disappointed if I couldn't pull this thing off. My fear of giving birth in a hotel suite paled in comparison.

It helped, I think, that I'm no stranger to less than ideal birthing situations. Sophia, my third and most impetuous child, came swimming out on the Feast of the Assumption in the back of our car, and Zelie, my fifth, was born in a small, unfamiliar cottage a state away from where we resided. The rest of my small enchanting creatures were born as planned, though some at home and some at the hospital. (I get kind of capricious when making birth plans.) Also, this baby boy we were expecting was our seventh child, so there was a slight chance I'd gotten a little overly confident in my birthing abilities.

HOW LONG, O LORD, HOW LONG?

They say that there are two kinds of women — the kind of woman who loves pregnancy but hates childbirth and the kind of woman who hates pregnancy but loves childbirth. I fall firmly into the latter category. Pregnancy and I share no love. Not even a smidgen.

I've always wished that I were one of those women who blossomed as new life took form beneath her ribs, a woman who savored and reveled in every last strange sensation. But life is not fair, and having lost the cosmic lottery of life, I ended up being more of a woman who swells and wilts rather than blooms and glows.

But childbirth? Oh, I love it. I love the promise of those first subtle contractions and the intimate moments shared between Dan and me as he supports me through the less subtle ones. I love the ecstasy of the moment of delivery, the relief of having been delivered of child (as the English so perfectly phrased it after Princess Kate gave birth), and the jubilant celebration that follows. All this is to say that all throughout the first and second trimesters I was ready and willing to give birth in that hotel if that was what God had in mind.

But as the weekend of the conference drew nearer and I grew larger, I began to worry about this birth in a way that I never had before. I was thirty-six years old, and bringing new life into the world in the second half of your thirties is a wholly different experience from that of growing a child in your twenties. I was more tired, the aches and pains were more burdensome, and somehow, even though I'd done this six times before, I felt more intimidated by the prospect of labor than I ever had before.

I've always taken great joy in preparing for birth. Whole Foods, for example, can count on me to drop a small fortune in their laps as I stock up on every essential oil and supplement that anyone has ever suggested might lead to a more blissful birth experience. Amazon and Trader Joe's can also count on having good financial quarters as I prepare to fill my house with candles, flowers, and delicious labor-friendly snacks. I spend hours choosing the perfect songs for my birth playlist while I wonder if this might be the child who finally gifts me with one of those elusive unicorn-like painless births we've all heard exist but have never actually experienced or seen with our own eyes.

This time around, though, I did none of that. I just kind of sat there, staring into space, feeling mildly apprehensive, and dreaming about the moment that I would be done, babe in my arms.

It didn't bode well.

Fortunately, I didn't have too much time to dwell on this troubling detour from my normal routine as four hundred women were about to descend on Charleston and had a reasonable expectation of finding a conference (and possibly a live birth experience) waiting for them when they arrived.

They got the conference but not the live birth experience, I am happy to report. It was touch and go there for a bit, though. To make things extra sanctifying, God thought it might be interesting to see what would happen if he allowed the ancient water system at the hotel to break down that weekend. Imagine this: you're forty weeks pregnant, tasked up to the gills at a conference that is taking place during an especially brutally hot and humid summer, and you can't take a shower. Or flush the toilet. (Nor can any of your guests.)

Thanks to the stress of that situation, and the fact that I was full to bursting with baby, I suppose, I spent much of the weekend in early labor, my body trying to kick things into gear only to decide it needed a siesta.

By the time I stumbled back into my house on Monday, I was a wreck. My body was so battered that I could barely walk, let alone see straight. The thought that labor was on the horizon filled me with panic, as there was absolutely no way my body could manage labor in its broken state.

Dan sent me to bed, where I passed out for almost eight hours. As the sun was setting, I awoke to an intense contraction ripping through my body. I struggled to breathe through it, curled in the fetal position. Tears flooded my eyes as I realized that I was going to have to labor through my first night back at home. To top it off, the kids had been sick with a stomach bug while I'd been away, so Dan was exhausted as well, and I just knew that there were evil germs lying in wait, ready to attack my innocent newborn. I was a wreck.

After a few more contractions came and went, I told Dan that I thought this was it and asked him to get everything ready. He fed the kids dinner, tucked them into bed, scrubbed the entire house from top to bottom and from bottom to top, and then came back to the bedroom where he found me decidedly not in labor. The contractions had stopped, and I was mortified.

It doesn't matter whether you're a first-time mom or a seventh-time mom, incorrectly calling the onset of labor is distressing. You've hyped yourself (and everyone else) up, you're ready to go, way past ready to meet your little one, and then nothing. On one hand I was relieved given how spent I was, but on the other hand, what was I going to do about the fact that I was never going to have this baby? I chose the only possible route and broke down into a messy heap of sobs in Dan's arms. Between having been on solo parenting duty with six vomiting children for four days, his regular work duties, and now with an inconsolable wife in his arms, I'm pretty sure he was silently praying for the Second Coming.

Lest you think that this story wraps up tidily with a quick and uncomplicated birth, let me save you the misery of a drawn-out melodramatic play-by-play and simply say this: the starting and stopping of my labor continued for six more miserable days. Six days of tears, six days of contractions, and six days of shaking my fist at God and wailing, "How long, O' Lord? How long?" It was fun for everyone.

A TRUE ADDITION

Active labor finally began on a sweltering Saturday morning — though I didn't know it at the time because my contractions continued to be agonizingly far apart and disorganized. It may have been due to this strange pattern that my newly developed fear of childbirth became even more intense. I couldn't have articulated what exactly it was that I feared, but I was overwhelmed by relentless anxiety. I sat in Dan's dark green armchair with tears streaming down my face. Never once before had I been anxious during labor, and I couldn't fathom where this fear was coming from. The fact that this experience of childbirth was completely different from my previous experiences only served, somehow, to heighten my anxiety.

Dan held me close and whispered soothing words in my ear. I begged him to pray with me, to ask God to please liberate me from this fear. Taking my hand in his, he knelt down before me and began to offer prayers of supplication. I joined in when I could, but even when words eluded me, I silently pleaded with God to bring relief.

He didn't say no. But he also didn't lift my anxiety.

Instead he said, "Your suffering is not without meaning, my girl. I am asking you to embrace it because it is through surrendering to this frightening, painful experience that you will heal another broken part of your soul and make space to welcome an even greater degree of my divine peace into your life."

Dan continued to pray, and God continued to speak. "Offer it up," God whispered, "Offer it up through me, with me, and in me. Unite your sufferings to my Holy Cross." I'll be honest with you. Ordinarily, such a prompting would probably have left me apoplectic, but after six experiences of childbirth I knew that God was right. I knew that the only way I was going to survive this experience was to take all of my pain, frustration, exhaustion, anxiety, and despair and lift it heavenward (or angrily throw it, as the case may be, and sometimes was).

It took me a long time to understand what it means to "offer up" our suffering. Why would God who is perfect and all-powerful — and clearly far better at handling this suffering business than I — need my pathetic offerings? What could I possibly have to add to his already perfect sacrifice upon the Cross?

I grappled with this issue for years, reading the writings of people far wiser than I am and quizzing anyone I could find who demonstrated a propensity for offering up their sufferings, but it never really clicked until I stumbled across a brilliantly simple explanation offered by Mother Miriam of the Lamb of God on her daily radio show.

> I was sharing with a group of women today a story that I have shared many times … that would help me — of thinking of a mother in the kitchen baking a chocolate cake. She has all of the ingredients. She is sufficient for the task. She needs nothing and she needs no one, but into the kitchen comes her little three-year-old daughter.

"Mommy, can I help you?"

And love receives. Love doesn't say, "No, goodbye. I have enough." Love receives.

And, so, the mother says, "Sure, honey."

And the little girl comes and throws some egg, or flour, or stuff in the cake. The mother didn't need her help, but the mother receives her addition. And, it's a true addition.

It is a true addition. How about that? God doesn't need my paltry offerings, but with arms outstretched upon the Cross he invites me, nevertheless, to cooperate with him. He allows me to throw heaping spoonsful of sugar into his divine cake and offers me the opportunity to take all of the prickly, unpleasant realities of my life and sweeten them by turning them into a force for good. In telling me to offer up my labor pains, he was giving me a gift. He was reminding me that my suffering is not something meaningless to simply be endured, but an opportunity to assist him in healing not only the world, but also myself.

Instead of remaining inwardly turned, focused solely on my own misery, this small act of offering up my suffering shifted my gaze outward and focused my thoughts on others. Suddenly, with the hope that I might be able to help others in some small way, I actually found myself wanting the contractions to intensify and to hurt a bit more.

The fear and anxiety continued to plague me through the long hours of labor, but in reminding me that my suffering had a purpose, and that he can and will bring good out of anything, God strengthened me and made me feel brave. Instead of resisting the pain, I was able to lean into it, and let me tell you, that is an entirely preferable way to experience suffering.

I became a woman at battle, in pursuit of a greater good and a deeper peace, rather than a helpless victim. Instead of feeling abandoned by God, I was cooperating with him. And through this shift in my perspective I was able, little by little and moment by moment, to surrender.

GAME-TIME DECISION

Apparently God looked down, saw me channeling St. Joan of Arc, and decided that I might find it fun to take on a little extra challenge. As the day drew to a close and I labored alone in my bathroom — under the false impression that I had hours of labor left to endure — a breathtakingly intense contraction ripped through my body, and Max began to descend. I could hear Dan in the hallway readying our children for bed and had to make a game-time decision. Do I start screaming and invite my entire family into the bathroom or do I deliver this baby by myself? Not wanting to traumatize my kids who were unprepared to witness birth at that moment, I chose the latter.

Once again, fear rushed through me as I attempted to push my son out into the world. Unlike my previous six children who had torpedoed out of my body with very little effort on my part, this child felt stuck. I'd been worried all week that he was malpositioned, thinking that maybe that was the reason for the extended start/stop pattern of my labor, and now I was even more concerned. A dear friend of mine had recently delivered a baby who was presenting posteriorly (face up) and described it as the single most terrifying, painful experience of her life. I suspected that my son was posterior as well, and without anyone to assist me with the birth, had no idea how I would manage.

Almost everything inside of me wanted to shut down and submit to fear's paralyzing spell, but that one glimmer of fierceness that rises above all else when your child is in danger took over and urged me on. I grit my teeth, handed off all of my pain and anxiety to God, and, all alone in my dim bathroom, I pushed with all my might. A few brutal minutes later, out came my "sunny side up" eight pound, fourteen ounce boy, God's newest little gift for the world, full of pure, delicious goodness.

We named him Max after St. Maximilian Kolbe, the saint who offered up his very body at Auschwitz to save the life of another.

CHAPTER THIRTEEN

Magnolias

**Darkness cannot drive out darkness;
only light can do that.**
~ *Martin Luther King, Jr.*

I took the roast out of the oven and poked at it. I wasn't exactly sure what "fall apart tender" was supposed to look like, but the meat seemed to shred easily enough, so I left it on the counter to "rest." It's hard work becoming "fall apart tender," apparently.

In the living room, candles were propped on every surface, sending light dancing across the walls. Harry Connick, Jr., serenaded me through our speakers while I set the table with the green and silver fine china Dan and I had been given for our wedding. A magnolia floated in a bowl of water in the middle of our dining table sending my thoughts back to the earliest days of my relationship with Dan.

****

"Have you ever smelled a Magnolia?"

I shook my head.

"Wait here."

Dan pulled the car over to the side of the road and jumped out. He ran up to a stately tree, its waxy leaves bowing to the ground, weighed down by large, buttery white blossoms. As he was known to do when performing with his band, he jumped high, stretching his ropey arm up to a branch barely out of reach. He plucked a flower and loped back to me.

I rolled down my window. He leaned in, gave me a kiss, and brought the blossom to my nose. "Smell this, my sweet girl." The scent was overwhelming in the most intoxicating, fragrant, vanilla-esque, sweet, and citrusy kind of way. It seemed to me to be the perfect flower.

"I had no idea how much I would love it here," I said. "I mean, I've been to the South before and have always enjoyed my visits, but I didn't know how much it would come to feel like home to me. I even love the humidity!"

"Now I know for sure that the heat has gone to your head. You hate the humidity."

"No, no, that's not true. I hate the mosquitoes, and I hate the roaches, and I hate the feeling of sweat dripping into my mascara when I'm trying to accomplish something, but I don't hate the humidity; I love it."

"I'm not convinced," he said with a laugh.

"It's true. You know why? Because I love the feeling of the ceiling fan breaking through the heavy air when I'm swaying back and forth on your porch swing. I love how when I wake up in the morning all my windows are covered with fog. And I love the sweet relief that comes with pressing a cold glass of lemonade against my hot cheek. I wouldn't have any of those things without the humidity, so see? I really do love it."

"Well good, then," Dan said. "If you're happy, I'm happy. That's all I want, you know. For you to be happy."

****

The timer in the kitchen began to ring, pulling me back into the present moment. The pecan pie was done. I placed it on a cast iron trivet next to the magnolia and sat down to wait for Dan to walk through the front door.

Dan had been working hard juggling a full-time job plus graduate school, and we hadn't had much free time to spend with one another over the last few months. I'd been planning this surprise romantic dinner for days. I'd poured the wine and prepared all of his favorite foods: pie, mashed potatoes, green beans, and even a roast. I say "even" because before I moved to the South and married Dan, I didn't have the faintest idea what to do with red meat.

My parents had been hippies when I was young, and my early years were spent eating vegetarian food. Eventually my mom added a little fish and poultry to our diet, and we would eat the odd hamburger while at restaurants, but I don't remember a single instance of my parents cooking red meat. This was of no small concern to my red-meat-loving southern-born-and-bred husband when we met, so here I was trying to create and identify "fall apart tender" pot roast.

I looked at the clock — 6:15 p.m. I'd been expecting Dan by 6:00 at the latest. Where was he?

6:30 … 6:45 … 7:00.

Still no Dan. I confirmed that he had left work, but since this was before either of us owned cell phones, I had no way to contact him while he was enroute to the house. I started to panic. It wasn't like him to be late without letting me know. My imagination ran wild as I waited for the police to knock on my door and deliver tragic news.

7:15 … 7:30 … 7:45.

Now I was just angry, imagining him deciding to go out for a drink with his brother or stopping by the bookstore on the way home without telling me. By the time he walked through the door shortly after 8:00 p.m., I was livid. As soon as I confirmed that he was alive and well, I left the food on the table, marched into our bedroom, slammed the door, and refused to speak to him for the rest of the night.

As I lay in bed that night, I tried to pinpoint the moment that Dan had stopped loving me. Was it before our recent wedding? After? On the way home tonight? And why? My heart alternately ached and raged.

By the time I woke up the next morning, he'd already left for work. On the kitchen counter was a note that said, "I'm so sorry, my girl. Let's talk tonight."

I spent the day cleaning up the mess left from creating the feast we had not consumed the night before. I missed Dan fiercely. I hated fighting with him but couldn't quite let go of the fact that he had so thoughtlessly and selfishly and heartlessly stood me up the night before. Despite what his note had said, it was clear that he didn't value our relationship or me and when presented with a few hours of free time would rather spend them without me. Our young marriage was clearly doomed.

By the time I heard the front door squeak open that evening, I'd catalogued a startlingly long list of all the things I suspected Dan might have preferred to do the night before rather than hang out with me. But the moment he walked up to me and lifted my downcast face in his hands, I burst into tears.

"I'm so sorry I wasn't here to enjoy your magnificent feast last night, my sweet girl. I was on my way home when

I saw a homeless man on the side of the road without a coat. It was so freezing last night that I just couldn't stand to not help him. Forgive me?"

"You don't need my forgiveness," I said. "I need yours — for not giving you the benefit of the doubt and for shutting you out last night. Forgive me?"

"Of course. Always."

FIGHTING TO LOSE

I was thinking recently about the early tumultuous days of our relationship — the days when everything that happened between us seemed so huge and important. Back then every hill was made to die on, and every slight seemed to point to a tragic deficiency in love. In truth, we were experiencing the ordinary ups and downs of life and marriage, but in my naiveté, they felt monumentally important and menacing.

I didn't know yet that Dan would spend the next decade pouring himself out, suffering, and sacrificing for me. I didn't know that he would gaze upon me at my weakest moments, with all my faults and flaws on full display, and see goodness hiding behind my imperfections. I didn't know that he would forgive me my every offense. And I didn't yet know that, when it came to my husband and our union, I had nothing to fear.

In the back of my mind, I was constantly waiting for Dan to fall out of love with me, walk away, and break my heart. Or if not that, then at the very least to grow apathetic toward me and cease to be delighted by our love. This fear ate away at me. It directed a pernicious spotlight at all of our interactions, leaving huge dark shadows dancing about in my mind that distracted me from the truth: that what we were experiencing were the normal growing pains of a young marriage.

We are a passionate couple — our love is fierce and so are our arguments. In the beginning, when we were still getting to know one another, learning each other's ways, and figuring out how to nurture a marriage, there were a lot of misunderstandings, and those misunderstandings led to a lot of explosive, destructive arguments. I needed constant reassurance that he still loved me in spite of our growing pains, and the fear that fed those doubts also led me to lash out as I sought reassurance.

We did battle weekly, sometimes daily. We seemed never to run out of things to argue about, and we failed to make any discernible progress in learning to fight fair or find peaceful resolutions to our differences. We fought only to win, which did nothing more than leave us both as losers. At the same time, we were both growing increasingly despondent by our apparent inability to foster a peaceful union. How's that for a vicious cycle? The more we fought, the more despondent we became; the more despondent we became, the more we fought.

Not anymore. We only very rarely fight, and the intensity is less. Our days are defined by a calm in our spirits. But not a dead calm! One that's fresh and cool, like a new season with new challenges to face and new lessons to learn.

Most of the credit for that goes to God, of course. I know many people expect me to follow a statement like that with a jaw-dropping anecdote about a particular day in our lives when God bestowed a miracle upon us that healed our troubled hearts in a single flash of lightning. The fact is, there is no one moment in our history when we looked at one another and made a commitment to lay our weapons down. That doesn't make it any less attributable to God's saving power. To borrow from G. K. Chesterton's *The Everlasting Man*, a slow miracle is not any less amazing than a swift miracle, and may actually "be rather more creepy and uncanny." And it *is* uncanny to look back and see how ridiculously far we've been able to come in spite of ourselves and realize that it was because God was working right in the midst of our battles, hearing our hateful words but also our hearts' desires for mercy and reprieve. In his incomprehensible goodness, he kept saying "yes" week after week: "Yes, I will infuse you with more love for one another than you ever could have imagined. Yes, I will tear down the silly walls that stand between you. And yes, you will have your happily ever after — though it may look a little different than your young, naive mind might once have imagined."

I can still remember the day I looked at our marriage and realized that at some indeterminate moment we had ceased to face life's challenges as individuals who believed that their best chance at survival was to protect themselves. Somewhere along the way we had learned that the best way to navigate the often rocky road of life was to care first for one another. The shift from being selfish to selfless, from being me-focused to other-focused, brought about a breathtaking transformation in our marriage. Though we still occasionally lose our tempers and fail to treat one another with patience and kindness, I still marvel at the metamorphosis.

INTO THE LIGHT

God is the Divine Healer, yes, but he is also the Divine Teacher. And while he was healing us, he was also teaching me a little something about fighting the fear that was attempting to destroy my marriage.

During the early years of my marriage I had very few friends. Not only had I recently moved across the country, leaving many friends behind, but I'd also converted to Catholicism, changing my entire worldview in the process. I struggled to know how to relate to my old friends, most of whom in addition to not being Catholic were not married. But I also had yet to form new relationships. It was a lonely time.

There are few things that can grow one's relationship with God faster than loneliness. During that season I spent a lot of time talking to him simply because I didn't have anyone else to talk to. I think God knew that I needed that time with him during those first years after my conversion, which is why, I suspect, he held off on bringing close friends into my life. I am, and always will be, grateful for that. The dark side of loneliness, though, is that I've always found it to be a rich breeding ground for spiritual attack.

Here's why: when it comes to my fears, my tendency is to keep them tucked away deep within me. I am ashamed of them. I am afraid of how others might react if I were to share their details. I am scared of them. And, at the end of the day, I would really rather not think about them at all if I can help it. So I shove them down so deep that not a ray of light can find them. There they eat away at me, feasting on the darkness and growing grossly out of proportion. There, with no one to argue with them, they convince me of their inerrancy and tell stories full of hopelessness, isolation, humiliation, and death. There, they win. But only there.

With my husband working forty-plus hours a week and going to classes in the evenings, and without a close friend to confide in, my fears had a field day. They damaged my marriage, impeded my spiritual growth, and left me almost constantly agitated and anxious to one degree or another.

And then God sent me a friend. The kind of friend who is really more of a sister. One day Jen was not there; the next she was, and it was as if she'd been there all along. From the very beginning, there was nothing I could not tell her and very few things she did not intimately understand.

Dan has always been an extraordinary confidant. He knows when to speak and when to stay silent. His advice is sage, and his perspective always merciful. But he's not a woman, a mother, a wife, or a convert to Catholicism. I am convinced that every woman needs a like-minded female friend or relative to confide in. I certainly know I do. Before Jen appeared in my life, I prayed for many years for her to arrive, and when she did I knew that God had been listening all along. The fruits of our friendship had God's fingerprints all over it.

Starting on the very first day we met, all of those fears that I'd been burying down deep inside of me came pouring out. Shame was destroyed with commiseration, lies with reality checks, and intimidation with the knowledge that I was no longer alone in my struggles. My fears had been brought into the light, where they ultimately didn't stand a chance.

Of course my fears, not content to be dismissed so easily, still like to whisper scary lies into my ear from time to time. That won't stop, I presume, this side of heaven. Sometimes I stumble and fall, and for a moment I believe them. Sometimes I even act on them.

A RETURN TO PEACE

Recently our family faced a huge financial challenge. Dan approached it with his usual steadiness and faith, which, under the influence of spiritual attack, enraged me. How could he remain so calm under the threat of such a catastrophic crisis? I let fear form my words and spewed all sorts of vitriol in his direction, and then I stomped out of the room.

I was almost immediately filled with regret. I may not always conquer spiritual attack, but I've become very good at recognizing it, and I knew at once that I'd given in to it once again. I knew what I had to do.

Head hung in shame, I walked back downstairs and apologized.

If I have learned anything over the past few years, it is that there is nothing more destructive to a relationship than the failure to apologize, to ask for mercy, and, in return, to offer it. With each failure to reconcile, grudges, hurt, and resentment become etched more and more deeply into your soul, eating away at your marriage and making healing and true reconciliation that much harder to bring about. I am convinced that these things have the potential to cause far more damage than anything that might occur during the short period of time in which angry words are exchanged: these wounds, if left untended to, have a tendency to fester and become infected. Because of this, Dan and I have made it a habit, albeit a painful one at times, to orient every action we take and every postargument thought that crosses our minds toward a return to peace.

Dan, being the merciful guy that he is, forgave me for the five-millionth time, and we were once again united in love and peace and ready to take on the world hand in hand.

All of these things — sharing your fears, allowing others to love and assist you, acknowledging your faults and asking for mercy, and offering forgiveness — they are all different branches of the same life-giving tree. They are all a means of yanking fear up and out of the darkness and submitting it to the light of Christ where it can and will be destroyed.

CHAPTER FOURTEEN

Spreadsheets

**And one has to understand that braveness is not
the absence of fear but rather the strength to keep
on going forward despite the fear.**

~ Paulo Coelho

As I write this, I am sitting in my new home. If ever there
was a turn of events that shouldn't have been — an outcome
that defied all the odds — it was this. This house was meant
for someone else. A retired couple, maybe. Or a couple with
a far more acceptable number of children. Certainly a family with a more confidence-inspiring bank account, at the
very least. That was my assessment, anyway.

This was not the first home we had occupied in
Charleston, South Carolina, and our move to the Holy City
almost four years ago was not the first time we'd relocated as
a family. If my count can be trusted, it was the eighth time
in our eleven years of marriage. Take a touch of wanderlust
and add to it an unstable job market, and you end up packing up quite a few U-Hauls.

We'd never had any trouble finding houses to live in
before our move to South Carolina. Our previous landlords
had all seemed fairly happy to have us occupy their homes
for a time. Some of them even became friends. I'm not sure
what changed when we moved to Charleston, but houses

that were move-in ready were suddenly becoming unavailable once we mentioned that we had five kids. One woman even said to us, "I wouldn't rent to a family with five dogs. I'm certainly not going to rent to a family with five kids." (Little did she know that I'd just found out I was expecting number six.)

I must have called and spoken with over twenty homeowners and real estate agents before I found one who was even willing to consider our rental application, and she was far from sold on us. She kept repeating over and over again, "I don't know. Eight people seems like an awful lot of people to squeeze into this house." And I assured her over and over again that 1,800 square feet was plenty of room for us, detailing for her exactly how I planned to spread out the kids between the rooms. I even sent her a photo of our family all dressed up for my son's First Holy Communion, which I thought was very clever considering that's the best we will ever look as a group. She remained unsure, though, and I continued to fret about where we would live.

Finally, after many interminable days, she called me and told me that although she had other interested parties, she couldn't get our family out of her head and had come to the conclusion that God was telling her to rent her home to us. We were overjoyed and more than a little bit relieved.

Our new home was perfect for us. It was in an established neighborhood with towering trees and winding roads. And it had all sorts of lagniappes like a screened-in porch, wainscoting in the dining room, and a Jacuzzi tub. I was smitten with it.

Smitten, but not entirely at peace. Our landlady had been clear from the start that this property was an investment. One that she had plans to cash in one day to help pay for her kids' college tuition. With her children quickly nearing college age, I knew that we wouldn't be able to stay in this house for long. I dreaded the day we would find out that we had to move, fearing that once again I'd knock on as many doors and that none would open. (Because apparently, God has only so many tricks up his sleeve.)

I felt like I'd come so far in my journey to overcome fear; and yet this fear of not being able to find a home to live in haunted me, literally leaving me unable to sleep at night on the occasions when the spiritual attack was at its worst.

I knew we wouldn't have enough in savings for a down payment on a house anytime soon (or ever), that the Charleston rental market was only growing more competitive with each passing year, and that our family size was only increasing. There was no way we'd be lucky enough to find someone willing to rent to us a second time around even if God himself came down from heaven and instructed them to do so.

This idea that God's providence is finite or somehow limited by worldly circumstances seems ridiculous when you say it out loud, but that's what makes fear so destructive. It has a way of making even its most absurd lies sound compelling in the dark of night or isolation of private thought.

SICK AND SICKER

For all of its wonderful qualities, the home we were renting kept springing leaks. First in my closet, then in the master bathroom, then in the kids' bathroom, then in the master bathroom again, and the kids bathroom again, and repeat. At first this was merely a nuisance. Naptimes would be interrupted to accommodate repairs, or we'd have to eat takeout for a couple of nights while the kitchen ceiling was repaired. This is a little tough and tiresome when you have small children, but not life-ruining. Then, about two years into our stay, my family started to get sick.

At first it simply seemed like we were in one of those seasons that all large families are familiar with where you can't catch a break. As soon as one virus leaves, another walks in. It's exhausting but not uncommon. I thought it was a little strange, though, when my kids started to get ear infections. I had a startling number of ear infections when I was young (ending only when I had tubes put in my ears), but none of my kids had ever had problems with their ears. Then I contracted pneumonia. And bronchitis. And finally asthma. My oldest son coughed constantly for no apparent reason, my two-year-old ended up covered with hives that even Benadryl couldn't touch, several of my kids developed recurring stomachaches, and my husband had a sinus infection that came and went for almost a year.

This was not normal. Of that I was sure. I began to suspect that we had a mold problem. The thing was, I didn't see mold, and I couldn't smell it either. There had been mold in my closet after the roof had sprung a leak shortly after we moved in. And more recently, a small amount had been found in our garage after our water heater had broken. Both patches had been taken care of, though, and had never come back. Our landlady had always been great about promptly making repairs when they were called for, but if you can't see mold and you can't smell it, it's a bit of a tough sell to ask someone to test for it given that testing for mold, as it turns out, is breathtakingly expensive. I was convinced, though. And the more sick my family became, the more strongly I felt that something had to be done.

Dan and I talked about whether we should consider looking for a new house, but we were in one of our leaner seasons and didn't have a lot of extra money to fund a move. I was still convinced that no one would rent to us, and we couldn't actually see or smell mold, so what if we were wrong? What if there was no mold? What if we were all strangely sick for some other reason entirely?

It's one of the worst feelings in the world to see your kids growing sicker and sicker and feel powerless to stop or fix it. There are few things that will drive you to your knees more swiftly. I'm not great about praying. God and I talk all day about all sorts of things, but when it comes to down-on-my-knees focused prayer time, there is no lack of room for improvement. But I prayed on my knees for this. I asked God to heal my little ones. To reveal the mold so that it could be dealt with or to somehow find us a new place to live. And then I just sat there, waiting for him to make a move, because I had absolutely no idea how to handle this situation or what to do next.

SPREADSHEET OF DOOM

A few days before Christmas, my seven-year-old daughter, Lucy, came running into the house with a letter in her hand. I knew what it said before she even handed it to me. It was from our landlords explaining that the time had come to cash in their investment, that they were selling the house, and that we had six weeks to move.

This would be the moment that a well-adjusted, holy person would gaze heavenward and thank the God who had clearly orchestrated this in answer to their prayers. Since I am neither particularly well-adjusted nor holy, I opted to let my fears have a field day instead. I immediately opened up a virtual spreadsheet in my mind and began to list all the reasons we were doomed:

1) When we first moved to Charleston, we only had five children. We now had seven.

2) Our income was lower than it was the last time we searched for housing.

3) Our college debt was nearly the same.

4) We had nothing in savings to fund a move.

5) The rental market in Charleston was incredibly competitive.

As soon as Dan got home that evening, I shared a dramatic detailed assessment of the situation with him. Not only was there a 0 percent chance that we would be approved to rent a house, but both of Dan's parents had recently passed and mine lived all the way across the country in California, so we didn't even have a basement to live in should we not find a new home within six weeks. No matter how you spun it, the situation was bleak.

Dan listened patiently, as he does, then gently took my hand and said, "You know, Hallie, a spreadsheet can't predict whether God is going to move a mountain."

As soon as the words left his mouth, I knew he was right. Yes, the challenges we were facing were, in fact, the size of a mountain, but mountains have nothing on the mercy of God. I'd spent the past decade of my life pouring huge amounts of time and energy into learning how to overcome fear and to trust in God. If this had taught me anything, it was that God is quite fond of moving mountains. How had I forgotten that so easily?

What was wrong with me? How pathetic could one person be? Had I learned nothing?

"I haven't been teaching you how to be fearless, my girl. I've been showing you how to overcome your fears. You know what you need to do."

Did I? Well, yes, I suppose I did. Dan and God were trying to remind me that I had something immovable to hold onto whenever the winds of anxiety picked up and threatened to unmoor me. It suddenly dawned on me that when God had encouraged me to embrace fearlessness years before, he had not been instructing me to eliminate fear from my life entirely — an exercise in futility, if there ever was one — but rather to learn how to stand bravely in the face of fear. He'd been teaching me, lesson by lesson, how to strip fear's paralyzing spell from my life, find freedom, and walk forward in spite of all anxiety. This housing situation was merely his latest challenge for me.

I resolutely pushed myself off the couch, stood back up, and made a decision to push on every door that was presented to me, no matter how unyielding I perceived it to be. If God put a door in front of me, I was going to try to open it. I had prayed for deliverance from the Mold House, and God had answered so surely that there must be a doorway somewhere through which we could pass.

GOD MOVES MOUNTAINS

The next day Dan went into work and shared our dilemma with a coworker. As it turned out, she had a friend who was a real estate agent and was willing to help us for free. We immediately began to search for our new home.

The first house we looked at was in a relatively new neighborhood full of families, with nature trails winding behind the houses and ponds dotting the many acres. Because it was slightly farther away from the city, it was slightly larger than our current home but not significantly more expensive. It was yellow with a red door, and I immediately fell in love with it.

I did not love the high application fee quite as much, though. There was something about writing a check for almost $100 (against a bank account that held barely that) that brought my spreadsheet of doom back to life. I couldn't see spending money that we really couldn't spare on an application that I knew would be denied. Dan reminded me, though, that I had committed to knocking on every door that presented itself to us, and our real estate agent seemed to believe that we had a decent shot at getting the house, so I filled out the application (the list of my children's names and birth dates spilling off of the front page and onto the back), wrote the check, submitted it, and waited.

This was a couple of days before Christmas, and only by the grace of God did I manage to put it out of my mind so that I could fully enjoy the holiday. Several of us were unable to attend Christmas Mass because of the never-ending illnesses that continued to plague our family, but Christmas still came, and my little ones' eyes lit up, and my husband and I kissed, and it was every bit as much of a joy-filled day as it ever was.

The following week Dan mentioned in passing that we should hear something about the house soon. I muttered under my breath that I already knew what the verdict was and went about my business. But later that day I walked into Dan's home office only to have him look up at me with a smile that spoke a million words about how much he loves me in spite of — and maybe even because of — my silly ways and say, "The house is ours."

Somehow, against all odds, we had been approved. I couldn't believe it.

And yet there was still one more mountain left to move. We, who lived paycheck to paycheck, had two weeks to come up with first and last months' rent plus a sizable deposit.

Impossible, I told God. And he laughed because what else is he going to do with me? But then he said, "Share your needs with your friends. Don't be afraid to be vulnerable. Don't be prideful. Let people love you."

And so I did. I told friends old and new what we were facing, and one person after another and another and another stepped up to help. A number of individuals donated to our moving fund, a women's group in Connecticut paid me a generous speaking fee to come and speak to their group that same month, a friend who creates beautiful products for mothers and their babies gave me the opportunity to earn a commission by reviewing her products online, another friend offered to lend us money, and unexpected checks began to arrive in our mailbox. It was the most generous outpouring of love that I have ever experienced.

When all was said and done, we had, down to the dollar, the exact amount of money we needed to move into our new yellow home with the red door. Dan had been right; my spreadsheet had failed to predict whether God would move a mountain. I remain convinced that anyone who had looked at the data would have agreed with me that with the rental market being as competitive as it was, and our application being as unimpressive as it was, the odds of our finding a suitable home were slim to none. Never in a million years would I have guessed that the first application we submitted would be accepted, that the home we applied for would be so perfect for us, and that everyone around us would lift us up, giving of their time, talent, and money, to get us into our new home. But it was, and it is, and they did.

A few days after we moved in, I was sitting on the couch with Dan at the end of the day when it suddenly struck me that none of our kids was sick. For the first time in over a year our home was free of stomachaches, coughs, rashes, headaches, runny noses, and ear infections. All of our tiny olive plants were tucked into their beds breathing easily and deeply with pink cheeks and full hearts.

I had asked God to save my children, and he had answered.

He had moved a mountain.

And he had shown me once again how to stand in the face of my fears, cling tightly to his steadfast love, and take courage.

Acknowledgments

To Hannah, Valerie, and Amanda: You three sweethearts have taught me that God brings the choicest blessings into our lives at the most surprising, unexpected times. Thank you. For everything.

To Liz Aiello, Adam Hamway, Jackie Resciniti, and the entire SiriusXM team: You gave me my first taste of radio (which is an exercise in summoning courage if ever there was one). Rarely have I had so much fun. Thank you for your guidance and encouragement.

To Melanie Shankle, Lino Rulli, Colleen Carroll Campbell, Leah Darrow, Patrick Madrid, Paul Thigpen, and Brandon Vogt: Thank you for your friendship and generous endorsements of this book. I think y'all are the bee's knees.

To Kimberly and Therese: Who knew South Carolina would bring such cutie pies into my life? May God grant us many more Margarita-themed outings.

To my editor, Cindy Cavnar: Thank you for your gentle nudges and wise counsel.

To Greg Erlandson: Thank you for believing in this book. It's been an honor to work with you.

To all my Edel Gathering gals: Thank you for the crazy shoes, tipsy toasts, wild karaoke nights, and everlasting sisterhood.

To Cate Roberts: Your words never fail to be a balm to my often weary, frustrated soul. Thanks for the love, support, and laughter. Your book is next! I know it's going to blow us all away.

To Joe Fulwiler: You're an original in the best sense of the word. Thank you for your friendship.

To my goddaughter, Pamela: I look forward to watching as you change the world. Stay fierce, sweet pea.

To Arwen: What a gift it has been to discover our faith together, my beautiful cousin.

To my grandmothers, Jane and Virginia: Life is a series of highs and lows. Thank you for teaching me how to weather the lows with grace and savor the highs with abandon. I love you both so much.

To Genie: You hold a very special place in my heart. Thank you for showing me that though life may be excruciatingly painful at times, we can emerge with tender hearts and a greater capacity to love.

To my sister: I wouldn't have been able to conquer nearly as many Feats of Bravery if you hadn't been by my side. Thank you for the camaraderie. (And that Blink-182 concert.)

To my mom: Thank you for the lovely roses, the care with which you chose them, and for all they have taught me.

To my dad: Thank you for always having faith in me. I wish I had the words to convey what an inestimable gift that has been.

To Jennifer Fulwiler: There's no one in the world with whom I'd rather build and board a rocket ship. I can't wait to see what adventures await us next.

To Daniel, Jack, Sophia, Lucy, Zelie, Charlie, and Max: You seven are the reason I smile in the morning, laugh during the day, and fall asleep with a heart full of gratitude at night. I love you with a tender fierceness I didn't know I possessed until you came along.

To my husband, Dan: Walking through life hand in hand with you is an incomparable privilege and delight. The Rockies may crumble, Gibraltar may tumble, but our love is here to stay. What a lucky girl I am.

To my merciful God: Thank you for taking me on this journey, patiently holding out your hand as I stumbled and fell over and over again, and for showing me that on the other side of fear lies freedom. Your love for me takes my breath away.

✶✶✶✶✶✶

And to everyone else who deserves my appreciation: If I haven't mentioned you, it is only because I have a terrible memory. But know that this book would not exist were it not for all the people who have loved and guided me over the years. Thank you. (Yes, you.)

About the Author

Hallie Lord is a bestselling author, popular speaker, Sirius XM radio host, and the co-founder of the Edel Gathering. She lives in South Carolina with her husband, Dan, and their seven enchanting children. You can connect with her at HallieLord.com.

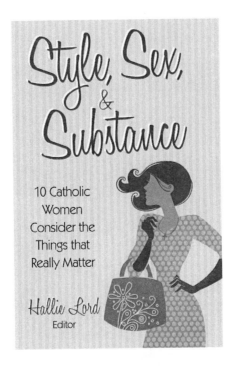